Stalingrad
The turning point

Geoffrey Jukes

Editor-in-Chief: Barrie Pitt
Art Director: Peter Dunbar

Military Consultant: Sir Basil Liddell Hart
Picture Editor: Robert Hunt

Design Assistants: Gibson/Marsh
Cover: Denis Piper
Research Assistant: Yvonne Marsh
Cartographer: Richard Natkiel
Special Drawings: John Batchelor

Contents

Stalingrad
The critical battle

Introduction by Captain Sir Basil Liddell Hart

Stalingrad was the most long drawn-out battle of the Second World War, and proved the most crucial. Geoffrey Jukes, who has made a distinguished mark as an expert on the Eastern Front, has written an account of this momentous struggle that is worthy of its theme.

After the narrow failure of Hitler's invasion of Russia in 1941 the German Army no longer had the strength and resources for a renewed offensive of that year's scale, but Hitler was unwilling to stay on the defensive and consolidate his gains. So he searched for an offensive solution that with limited means might promise more than a limited result. No longer having the strength to attack along the whole front, he concentrated on the southern part, with the aim of capturing the Caucasus oil – which each side needed if it was to maintain its full mobility. If he could gain that oil, he might subsequently turn north onto the rear of the thus immobilised Russian armies covering Moscow, or even strike at Russia's new war-industries that had been established in the Urals. The 1942 offensive was, however, a greater gamble than that of the previous year because, if it were to be checked, the long flank of this southerly drive would be exposed to a counterstroke anywhere along its thousand-mile stretch.

Initially, the German *Blitzkrieg* technique scored again – its fifth distinct and tremendous success since the conquest of Poland in 1939. A swift break-through was made on the Kursk-Kharkov sector, and then General Ewald von Kleist's 1st Panzer Army swept like a torrent along the corridor between the Don and the Donetz rivers. Surging across the Lower Don, gateway to the Caucasus, it gained the more westerly oilfields around Maikop in six weeks.

The Russians' resistance had crumbled badly under the impact of the *Blitzkrieg*, and Kleist had met little opposition in the later stages of his drive. This was Russia's weakest hour. Only an instalment of her freshly raised armies was yet ready for action, and even that was very short of equipment, especially artillery.

Fortunately for Russia, Hitler split his effort between the Caucasus and Stalingrad on the Volga, gateway to the north and the Urals. Moreover when the first attacks on Stalingrad, by Paulus's 6th Army, were checked in mid-July – although narrowly checked, Hitler increasingly drained his forces in the Caucasus to reinforce the divergent attack on Stalingrad. This was by name, 'the city of Stalin' so Hitler could not bear to be defied by it – and became obsessed by it. He wore down his forces in the prolonged effort to achieve its capture, losing sight of his initial prime aim, the vital oil supplies of the Caucasus. When Kleist drove on from Maikop towards the main oilfields, his army met increasing resistance from local troops, fighting now to defend their homes, while itself being depleted in favour of Paulus's bid to capture Stalingrad.

At Stalingrad the Russians' resistance hardened with repeated hammering, while the directness, and consequent obviousness, of the German attacks there simplified the Russian Higher Command's problem in meeting the threat. The Germans' concentration at Stalingrad also, and increasingly, drained reserves from their flank-cover, which was already strained by having to stretch so far – nearly 400 miles from Voronezh along the Don to the point where it nears the Volga at Stalingrad, and as far again from there to the Terek in the Caucasus. A realisation of the risks led the German General Staff to tell Hitler in August that it would be impossible to hold the line of the Don as a defensive flank, during the winter – but the warning was ignored by him in his obsession with capturing Stalingrad.

The Russian defenders' position there came to look more and more imperilled, even desperate, as the circle contracted and the Germans came closer to the heart of the city. The most critical moment was on October 14th. The Russians now had their backs so close to the Volga that they had no room to practise shock-absorbing tactics, and sell ground to gain time. But beneath the surface, basic factors were working in their favour. The German attackers' morale was being sapped by their heavy losses, and a growing sense of frustration, so that they were becoming ripe for the counter-offensive that the Russians were preparing to launch – with new armies, against the German flanks which were held by Rumanian and other allied troops of poorer quality. This counter-offensive was launched on November 19th.

Wedges were driven into the flanks at several places, so as to isolate Paulus's 6th Army. By the 23rd the encirclement was complete, more than quarter of a million German and allied troops being thus cut off. Hitler would permit no withdrawal, and relieving attempts in December were repulsed. Even then Hitler was reluctant to permit the 6th Army to try to break-out westward before it was too late, and air supply had proved inadequate.

The end came – the end of a battle of over six months' duration – with the surrender of Paulus and the bulk of what remained of his exhausted and near-starving army on January 31st, although an isolated remnant in a northerly pocket held out for two days longer.

Geoffrey Jukes's book benefits from his extensive knowledge of Russian sources, especially the six-volume History of the *Great Patriotic War of the USSR*, as well as the memoirs of some of the military leaders that have been published since then.

That official history provided much more factual evidence than the purely propagandist accounts published in the wartime and early post-war years. It corrected the absurdly exaggerated picture of Stalin's dominant influence on the struggle previously prevailing. But it should be borne in mind that the revised account was produced in Kruschev's period and with his backing – so that it tended to emphasise, and over-emphasise, his influence on the Stalingrad struggle while belittling that of Stalin. Moreover the influence of Marshal Zhukov, which had been relegated to the background in Stalin's time but was becoming mentioned afresh after Stalin's death, was again being put in the shade by Kruschev and his sychophants. Since Kruschev's overthrow it has come to receive its due share of recognition, following the publication, in 1965, of a one-volume history that while summerising the earlier six-volume history considerably revised its content and conclusions. Moreover Zhukov himself was allowed, or even encouraged, to produce his own memoirs, and these, significantly, contradict a number of assertions in Marshal Chuikov's earlier account of the Battle of Stalingrad.

This long process of tampering with history, and perverting it for propagandist aims, should be borne in mind when studying narratives and statements from Russian sources. It also compels caution in regard to any figures of strength or casualties given in them, even though they may appear more factual than the broader figures published earlier.

'Why Stalingrad?'

The great plain of Europe stretches from the coast of the English Channel across the Low Countries, Germany, Poland, and the Soviet Union to the foothills of the Urals. Occasionally, as if about to change its character, it gathers into the folds of undulating hills, but always it subsides again into monotonous flatness. Bounded on the north by the sea, and on the south – at least until the Ukraine – by mountains, it has for centuries been the stage on which first the tribes of Europe, Celt, Teuton, and Slav, then the fanatics of religion, and finally the more formalised, but no less warlike, armies of the national states which succeeded them, have enacted the gory dramas in which European history so deplorably abounds.

Inevitably in the absence of commanding heights, the most important defensive barriers of the plain are its great rivers – Rhine, Elbe, Oder, Vistula, Bug, Dvina, Dniestr, Dniepr, Don, Volga, and their tributaries – which flow across it to north or south. And it was on the banks of the mightiest of these, the Volga, and its scarcely less great neighbour, the Don, that the great complex of battles known to history as 'Stalingrad' took place in late 1942 and early 1943. Here where the immense cornfields of the Ukraine give way to the ravines and gullies of the Volga basin, the armies of two militant ideologies clashed in a fight for possession of a city, not originally considered a prime military objective, but which by the symbolism of its name and the doggedness of its defence came to dominate the efforts of both sides, and brought the Nazi attempt to forge an Empire in the East crashing down in ruins.

Not that this was the first time the Red Army had brought the Germans to a halt. The irresistible tide of German conquest had poured over European Russia throughout the summer of 1941, as it had over Western Europe in the previous year, and division after division of the ill-equipped, ill-trained, and ill-led Red Army had experienced the fate of the Poles, French, Dutch, Belgians, Yugoslavs, and Greeks – encirclement and capture. For them there had been, too, the additional cross of barbaric ill-treatment at the hands of their cap-

The Road to Stalingrad: German panzer in the drive to the Don

tors, as the Soviet Union was not a signatory of the Geneva Convention on treatment of war prisoners, and besides, the Russian shared bottom place with the Jew in the obscene racial pecking order of the Nazis, at the pinnacle of which stood the 'Herrenvolk' – the Master Race; German, of course. Thus the German respect for legality, which at its best ensured reasonably correct treatment for those in Western Europe and Scandinavia, but at its worst showed a tendency to exalt the letter of the law above its spirit, met in the East in unholy wedlock.

There were no legal bars to the application of Nazism in its full horror to the helpless masses of Russian prisoners, and in the camps they died in their hundreds of thousands. About 5,500,000 officers and men of the Red Army were captured in the course of the war, three-quarters of them in 1941, and about 4,000,000 of them were dead before the war reached its end. Treatment of the civilian population was little better, particularly once the German army had moved on to the east and been succeeded by the civil administration with its apparatus of Gestapo, special (execution) teams and concentration camps.

The result had been in the occupied areas to stifle enthusiasm for Nazism as a deliverance from the horrors of the Stalin regime, and in the unoccupied areas to quicken the will to resist, for at least the draconian severities of Stalinism were tempered by the promise of a better future, and some signs of this had already begun to appear in the form of the industrial revolution wrought under the Five-Year Plans. Stalin chastised them with whips, but Hitler with scorpions, and Nazism offered for the Slav no future other than that of a he... the German farming colonies which were to be established in the East as the granary of the 'Thousand-Year Reich'.

Though many individuals would collaborate with the Germans because they believed a German victory inevitable, or because of the personal hardships they had suffered from Stalin's communism, or to feed their families, or be rid of the Russian yoke (this last consideration was particu-larly strong among some of the non-Russian minorities which make up more than a third of the Soviet population), for the bulk of the Russians the home-grown dictatorship was much the lesser of two evils; and as evidence of Nazi atrocities was skilfully publicised by the Communist Party, and concessions were made to foster patriotism and recruit religious feeling for the cause, the Soviet resistance hardened and the population rallied round the figure of Stalin as they had never done in peacetime.

So despite brilliant victories in the field in the summer and autumn of 1941, the Germans found the Red Army and the Stalin regime still untoppled as the winter approached. Of the three major objectives – Leningrad, Moscow, and Kiev, the first two were still untaken when the winter approached, and what was more ominous, the handling of Soviet troops by their senior commanders was noticeably getting better, as the old Stalinist war-horses were shunted away to the rear and their place taken by younger men with a more up-to-date outlook and better professional grounding in the military art.

Among these the most outstanding figure was undoubtedly the ex-Chief of General Staff, Army General Georgy Konstantinovich Zhukov, and it was his decisiveness and ability to enforce his personality on events which now brought him to the fore. In October 1941, Stalin sent him to Leningrad, where in a three-day whirlwind of activity he organised order out of the chaos of the defence organisation, and imposed a solution which in the hands of others proved capable of withstanding a siege of more than 900 days. From there he was summoned urgently back to Moscow, which was in imminent danger of capture, and here his actions and advice as commander of West Front (the Army Group defending the city) and as a member of Stavka (the General Headquarters) not only succeeded in fending the Germans off from the capital, but exploited the weather and the German exhaustion to improvise a counteroffensive which flung the Wehrmacht right back on its heels, brought its

General Georgy Konstantinovich Zhukov

11

The first Winter in Russia caught the Germans too thinly clad

Army Group Centre to the brink of disintegration, and inflicted on Germany its first major defeat on land in the entire war. Never after this was the German army able to mount a strategic offensive along the entire front as it had done in 1941.

But eventually the Zhukov offensive petered out for lack of resources, and both sides paused to take stock. For the German generals, the experience seems not to have been fully digested. They could rationalise the defeat as being due to Hitler's vacillations over priorities, or to the mud of autumn or to the snow and ice of the winter – as if Stalin had never handicapped the Red Army's generals by vacillation or wrong decision, as if the autumn rain and winter snow had not fallen on *Herrenvolk* and *Untermensch* alike; and as if the sending of German troops on an essentially high-speed mobile operation in weather which froze their lubricants solid so that their vehicles would not move, so that their guns could not be fired until each shell or

cartridge had been individually scraped clear of the frozen grease which made it too large for the breech, was not in itself a negation of good generalship for which they were themselves responsible.

If the Soviet troops were properly clad for the winter, while the Germans were not, this was somehow to be laid at someone else's door. It was as if Stalin, with his passion for secrecy, had managed to conceal not only the strength of the Red Army's reserves, but the severity of the Russian winter; anyway, when the good campaigning weather returned in the spring, it would all be different. It had not been Soviet generalship which won the Moscow battle for them, it had been 'General Winter' with some help from the Führer; and in the meantime, German troops had gained some useful experience of defensive fighting which had been lacking from their offensive-minded training.

So reassured the German generals, missed the main lesson of the winter campaign – that the entire campaign in the East depended on overcoming

the Red Army before it developed the ability to cope with fast-moving armoured warfare, and that in essence this meant overcoming it before the winter of 1941. Already there had been evidence that the ruinous Soviet attempts to stand fast, with the inevitable consequence of encirclement, were being abandoned under the influence of better thinking stimulated by manpower shortage, and that when the Russians had fully absorbed the lessons of the summer (Zhukov undoubtedly had, as was shown by his order during the Moscow counteroffensive which categorically forebade frontal attacks against strongpoints, enjoining the use of by-passing tactics instead), the Red Army would, in the new campaigning season, prove harder to catch.

For its part, the Soviet leadership, and Stalin in particular, over-estimated the significance of the change in the strategic balance, just as the Germans underestimated it, and planned to follow up Zhukov's success with a strategic offensive along the whole front; and it was on January 5th, 1942, that the chain of

decision which made the Battle of Stalingrad inevitable really began to be forged. On that day Zhukov was summoned from his headquarters of West Front (in Soviet military parlance 'Front' means an Army Group) to a meeting of Stavka, at which future operations were to be considered; and here Stalin propounded a plan for a general offensive along the entire front between Leningrad and the Black Sea.

Zhukov knew that although the Germans had just taken a nasty beating in the centre, and a lesser one in the south, they were still a strong and dangerous enemy, and he argued for a strong offensive confined to the centre, where the German Army Group Centre was in greatest disarray. But Stalin's mind was made up, and at the end of the meeting the Chief of General Staff, Marshal Shaposhnikov, told Zhukov 'You were wasting your time arguing; the Supremo had already decided. The Directives have already been issued ..'

'Then why did he ask for our opinions?'

'I don't know, my dear chap, I don't know', said Shaposhnikov, and sighed. He did not favour the general offensive either.

A few days later the offensive was launched, but nowhere could it be strong enough to ensure success. Everywhere it failed; in places it led to disaster, with more armies squandered, and the Red Army left that much weaker to face the summer, worse still, the shaky morale of the German army was restored as it fought its first large-scale defensive actions of the war, and acquired experience which its offensive-oriented training had not given it. Thus the Red Army lost its chance of a breakthrough in the centre, and a further summer campaign on Soviet territory became inevitable. Both sides began to plan their offensives, and both selected the southern sector of the front for their main attacks.

The winter's fighting had left the front line very convoluted in shape; Leningrad was besieged, part of the Crimea was still in Soviet hands, and south of Kharkov was a large bulge in the line known as the 'Barvenkovo salient'. Thus the Stavka plan was for

13

the relief of Leningrad and the besieged Crimean fortress and naval base of Sebastopol, coupled with a major attack out of and north of the Barvenkovo salient, the last of which was to be the centre-piece of the entire summer offensive and was to aim at the recapture of Kharkov. It was to be conducted by forces from two Army Groups – South-West and South Fronts – under the command of Marshal S. K. Timoshenko, a Civil War veteran, who had become People's Commissar for Defence after the débacle of the winter war with Finland and carried out a ruthless reorganisation of the Red Army.

The offensive out of the Barvenkovo salient was to take the form of a pincer movement by 6th Army (Lieutenant-General A M Gorodnyansky), which was to strike out of the north face of the salient heading for Kharkov. From the Volchansk area north-east of the city, Lieutenant-General D I Ryabishev's 28th Army, with elements of the adjacent 21st and 38th Armies, would move down to meet 6th Army. A combat group commanded by Major-General L V Bobkin would thrust west out of the salient towards Krasnograd to protect the rear of 6th Army as it headed north. And to ensure that German forces on the south face of the salient were kept busy the 9th Army (Major-General F M Kharitonov) and 57th Army (Lieutenant-General K P Podlas) were to mount limited offensives designed to pin them down.

The plan was a fairly predictable one, given the shape of the front line and Kharkov's importance, both as the second largest Soviet city in German hands and as a main centre of German communications and supply in the south. That, however, was not necessarily fatal to its success; many less imaginative moves have been successful given the right conditions. Its really fatal flaw was more basic; it fitted, as if by design, into the German plans.

Hitler's design for the summer was much more ambitious than Stalin's, but before it could be put into effect the Wehrmacht had some preliminary operations to carry out. The Soviet bridgehead in the Crimea was to be eliminated; so was the Barvenkovo

salient. Consequently, as Timoshenko began to pack the salient with assault forces (including about 600 tanks, two-thirds of his total armour) so Field-Marshal Fedor von Bock, commanding Army Group South, was concentrating most of his VI Army (Colonel-General Friedrich von Paulus) against its north face, and assembling his I Panzer Army (Colonel-General Ewald von Kleist) opposite the southern neck of it, at Barvenkovo, In short, Timoshenko's best weapons - his T-34 medium and KV-1 heavy tanks, superiors of any German tank - were being committed to a punch into thin air against the lightly-held eastern face of the salient, while the real threat developed behind them in the form of 'Operation Fridericus' - the sealing off of the salient.

Neither commander realised what the other was up to, and had Bock been ready to go before Timoshenko's

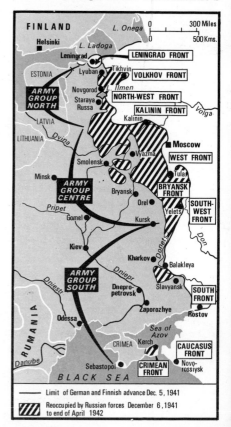

FINLAND

Limit of German and Finnish advance Dec. 5, 1941

Reoccupied by Russian forces December 6, 1941 to end of April 1942

Russia's great asset was superiority in quality of armour. The capability of the T34 came as a shock to the Germans in the early stages of Barbarossa. Later, the KV1 was to prove as effective

T-34 Medium. *Top:*
Weight: 32 tons. Speed: 33 mph. Armour (max): 1.8 inches at 60°. Crew: 4.
Armament: 1 x 76.2mm gun. 2 x 7.62mm mg

KV-1. *Bottom:*
Weight: 52 tons. Speed: 22 mph. Armour (max): 4.5 inches front. Crew: 5.
Armament: 1 x 76.2mm gun. 3 x 7.62mm mg

tanks were launched into the void, his Army Group South might have found itself in serious trouble; but in fact Timoshenko opened his offensive on May 12th, 1942, about a week before Bock was ready. At first, Timoshenko's southern pincer appeared to be going well (although the northern one was in difficulty from the outset) and the only snag from Timoshenko's point of view was that the tank brigades of his southern force did not seem to be encountering much opposition. Where had the Germans gone?

The question was answered on May 17th when probing patrols, sent out to establish the identity and strength of the German forces on the southern flank, came back with prisoners from I Panzer Army. Realising that he had walked into a trap and that with every hour that passed his armies were rolling deeper into danger, Timoshenko telephoned Stavka, and sought permission to slow down the offensive while he regrouped to meet the new threat. Permission was refused. Kharkov must be recaptured.

The Soviet offensive had not been without its effects on Bock's peace of mind. 'Fridericus' had been meant as a standard two-pronged operation with thrusts from both north and south to pinch out the neck of the salient, but it could no longer be carried out as such, because the northern neck, at Balakleya which was held by the XLIV Infantry Division (a Viennese division of the former Austrian Army) was under very heavy Soviet pressure; it was by no means certain that it could be held, and certainly no offensive could be mounted from there.

With some trepidation Bock therefore decided on a one-armed 'Fridericus', carried out solely by I Panzer Army from the south side of the salient, with infantry support provided by XVII Army. A force of two Panzer, one motorised, and eight infantry divisions was therefore assembled south of Barvenkovo, and hurled into battle on the morning of May 17th, one day earlier than the two-pronged 'Fridericus' had been due to start. There was some initial difficulty in breaking through the Soviet positions, but by the afternoon of the 22nd, XIV Panzer Division had reached

the south bank of the northern Donets at Bayrak, opposite the hard-pressed Austrians of XLIV Division. The pocket was closed and inside it was most of Timoshenko's assault force, for though he had managed on the 19th to obtain Stavka's permission to abandon the offensive and had sent his deputy, General Kostenko, forward to organise the withdrawal, Kleist had moved too fast for him.

Some Red Army units managed to fight their way out to the east, but most of the forces in the pocket were cut to pieces, 29 Soviet divisions were shattered, and many others severely mauled. Three armies had ceased to exist – 6th, 9th, and 57th, together with their commanders, except for Kharitonov and his HQ of 9th Army, who were flown out at the last moment; Kostenko was dead; Bobkin and his assault group were no more; 9th Army, which had under Kharitonov acquired an enviable record in the defensive battles of the previous autumn, would be sorely missed in the prolonged defence which would follow; two-thirds of the tanks were gone.

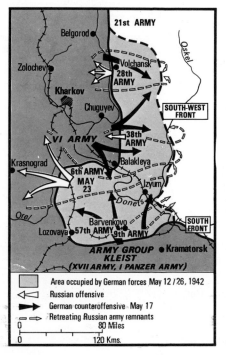

Area occupied by German forces May 12 / 26, 1942

◁— Russian offensive

■► German counteroffensive May 17

▭ ⇢ Retreating Russian army remnants

0   80 Miles

0   120 Kms.

And this had been only a tidying-up operation; the main German offensive was yet to come!

Many of the German generals had been opposed to the invasion of the Soviet Union, especially with the unsubdued British at their back and the likelihood that Britain would in due course provide the bases for an invasion of the Continent, and of the war on two fronts which Germany so dreaded. Since the ambitious 1941 plan with its offensive along the entire front, had brought neither the promised annihilation of the Red Army nor the collapse of the Stalin régime, the planners had to look more closely at the military, political, and economic premises of the war in deciding where to mount their major effort with their now more limited forces. Hitler, too, was preoccupied with political and economic realities – since the failure of the *Blitzkrieg* in 1941 inevitably committed Germany to a prolonged war, in which she now had three major industrial powers ranged against her, including the greatest colossus of all, the United States.

In the summer and autumn of 1941, Stalin's régime had withstood shocks greater than those which had toppled the régime of the Tsars in the First World War. Apart from the reasons already discussed, and perhaps more apparent to Hitler than to any of his generals, was the fact that industrialisation had endowed Stalin with sinews of war such as no Tsar had ever had. Much of the new industrial might of Russia – in particular the great steel plants of the Urals such, as those at Magnitogorsk – as out of Germany's reach for the foreseeable future, and the Soviet ability to produce tanks there was being supplemented by machinery evacuated from western industrial areas before the Germans arrived. In aircraft, too, Soviet production was rising steadily.

Thus, as *Blitzkrieg* tactics had failed in 1941, the longer the Russian Bear remained unkilled, the more likely it was that he would eventually overthrow his antagonist, especially now that much of America's industrial might was behind him.

But the Russian economic colossus had a very marked Achilles' heel, in that Soviet oil was mainly in the Caucasus, and from the oilfields of Maikop, Grozny, and Baku there were only a handful of routes by which it could reach distribution centres and eventually move the wheels and tracks of the Red Army. There was the rail link through Rostov. There was another, branching off the first at Tikhoretsk and making its way to Stalingrad, and a third went along the western shore of the Caspian Sea from Baku to Grozny, and on to Astrakhan where it linked up with a line to Central Russia. Last and most important was the mighty Volga itself, along which the huge oil-barges plied direct from Baku.

Capture Rostov, and the first route was cut. Take Maikop and Grozny, which were north of the Caucasus mountains, and the second and third rail routes would be severed. Establish troops on the west bank of the Volga, and the last route would be cut, killing the Soviet economy and bringing the Red Army to a halt. Better still, if the Caucasus was crossed and Baku captured, Soviet oil would turn Germany's wheels and make it possible for her to withstand a prolonged war, without having to depend on the Rumanian oilfields at Ploesti – vulnerable as they were to attack by Soviet bombers from the Crimea (until the Soviet bridgehead there was eliminated), or longer-range British or American aircraft from the Middle East.

Even by themselves, these were persuasive reasons for Hitler to place the emphasis of his 1942 campaign on the south; but there were others. Germany had both feet firmly planted in the western part of the Kharkov industrial area, but the eastern part – the coal and steel of the Donbass – was still under Soviet control. A drive to the Volga would rip straight through it, adding it to Germany's sources of military-industrial power.

Furthermore, there were great political benefits to be reaped from success in the south. Turkey might be induced to abandon her neutrality, for though her government's policy was generally pro-Allied, there was a great deal of goodwill there for Germany, based largely on the comradeship in arms of the First World War. By defeating the hereditary enemy of

Turkey and appearing on the Turko-Soviet border; furthermore, by cutting the supply route from America to the Soviet Union which passed through Iran, and thus threatening the Anglo-Soviet control of that country, Germany would become a power in the Middle East – able, if the Turks would play, to threaten the entire British position in that part of the world by advancing on the oilfields of the Persian Gulf and on the Suez Canal, to take the British 8th Army in the rear.

These, of course, were long-term considerations. In early 1942 the task confronting the German military planners was the more modest, though still formidable problem, of gaining the positions which would enable them to realise the glittering

Stalingrad: ... the natural place to anchor the eastern end of the flank defence line ...

prospects already moving in Hitler's lively though disordered imagination. Germany's forces were already considerably extended in maintaining the existing front line after the losses of the winter battles. A move south-eastwards against the Caucasus would extend the front line even more; the forces sent down into that area would not be available for quick redeployment in the event of trouble elsewhere on the front, and, furthermore, they would be presenting their rear to any Soviet riposte which might take the form of a north-south thrust along the Don towards Rostov.

If that should happen, they would either be cut off or would have to make a hasty retreat out of the Kuban and Caucasus. It was therefore necessary to set up a flank and rear guard to cover them against this danger, and the question was where this guard should be placed, bearing in mind that

Germany's forces were very stretched and her allies, Rumania, Italy, and Hungary, with their relatively poorly-equipped, badly trained and doubtfully enthusiastic forces, would have to take part in the operation.

The ideal line emerges even from a cursory glance at the map. South of the major communications centre of Voronezh, the Don begins to bend eastwards. It continues thus until east of Serafimovich, where it turns south before finally resuming a westerly course to its mouth in the Sea of Azov. The Volga, on the other hand, bends westward between its mouth at Astrakhan and Stalingrad. Thus any defensive line based on the Don would have the river in front of it to a point east of Serafimovich, and from there to the Volga is less than fifty miles. Only over this stretch could the Red Army attack without first making an opposed crossing of a major river, and

hence the natural place to anchor the eastern end of the flank defence line was the Volga, in the Stalingrad area.

Here the river is about a mile wide. Traffic on it could be disrupted by air or artillery bombardment, and any Soviet attempt to attack across the river would be hampered by the width of the water obstacle presented by it. There was no need to take the city; cut off from the north, accessible only by river boats under constant artillery and aircraft fire, it would be indefensible.

So no particular plan was made to take it. As Kleist said after the war 'At the start Stalingrad was no more than a name on the map to us', and the way the city graduated from its supporting role in the drama, and gradually usurped the lead, is shown in Hitler's statements and Directives as the year wore on, and as the political, economic, and military

factors battled for supremacy in his brilliant but warped mind.

The basic plan for the summer, drafted during the preceding winter by the Army High Command (*Oberkommando des Heeres*, or OKH) had envisaged only a modest campaign in the south. The centrepiece was to be in the north, in the capture of Leningrad and a link-up with the Finns. The plan was rejected, but the Leningrad operation remained in all the drafts which followed, and this fact was in due course to influence the fighting far away on the Volga.

On March 28th the Chief of General Staff of OKH, Colonel-General Franz Halder, a brilliant planner who was unusual in being a product not of the Prussian General Staff, but of the old Bavarian army (and perhaps even more unusual in that, unknown to Hitler, he had been a key figure in an abortive plot to assassinate him in 1938), presented the revised operational plan for the summer offensive at a conference held at Hitler's headquarters, the *Wolfs-schanze* (Wolf's Lair) deep in the gloomy forests of East Prussia near Rastenburg. It was code-named *Fall Blau* (Case Blue – there had been a reversion to the use of colours for code-names since the failure of the great exception 'Barbarossa') and envisaged a two-stage offensive.

It was unusual in that it was to be mounted from a backward-slanting line, and therefore the first force to move would be that which started from the furthest point west. This would drive south-east along the Don from the Kursk-Kharkov area, herding Timoshenko's armies away from the river and getting round behind them, and then, at the appropriate moment, the force at the southern and eastern end of the line would move out due east from the Mius river, shepherding the Soviet South Front away to north and west. The two forces would meet west of Stalingrad, encircling and wiping out the whole of the Soviet South-West and South Fronts, to bring the first phase of the operation to a successful conclusion, and only then would they swing south towards the Caucasus and the oilfields.

Hitler accepted the plan, but rejected the Directive into which it was translated, and insisted on drafting it himself, making it much more specific than usual (a Directive normally laid down the objectives but left the details of their attainment to the commanders concerned, but Hitler mistrusted his generals, especially since the winter débacle).

The result, Directive No. 41 of April 5th 1942, therefore gives a very good picture of Hitler's thinking at the time. In it he said 'it is fundamentally necessary to unite all available forces for conduct of the main operation in the southern sector, with the aim of

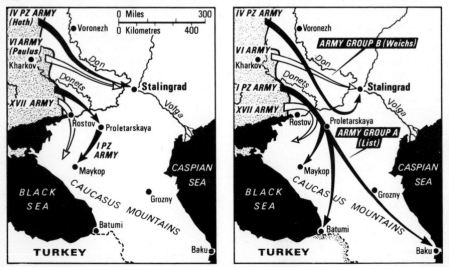

20 *Fall Blau:* left Halder's version, right Hitler's version

destroying the enemy west of the Don, so as subsequently to capture the oil regions in the Caucasus and cross the Caucasus range'. He also said 'in any event, an attempt must be made to reach Stalingrad itself, or at least to remove it from the list of industrial and communications centres by subjecting it to the action of our heavy weapons . . .' The emphasis was clear. It was 'fundamentally necessary' to destroy the Soviet forces in the south, and then take the oilfields; but 'an attempt' must be made to take Stalingrad *or bring it within range of heavy guns or bombers.*

Bock was given formidable forces for the operation. For the northern pincer along the Don he had IV Panzer Army (Colonel-General Hermann Hoth) and VI Army (Colonel-General Paulus); for the southern, I Panzer Army (Kleist) and XVII Army (General Richard Ruoff), while XI Army (Colonel-General Erich von Manstein) would also be available once it had cleared the Crimea and captured the fortress of Sebastopol. Satellite forces under command of Army Group South would consist of III and IV Rumanian, VIII Italian, and II Hungarian Armies, and the total forces under Bock's command thus came to 89 divisions, nine of them armoured.

In early May 1942, the two Soviet 'Axes' (headquarters controlling more than one Army Group) in the south – South-West and North Caucasus – had between them 78 divisions (14 of them cavalry) and 17 tank brigades, which on the face of it was an adequate force with which to defend their area.

But these figures have to be interpreted with some care. First of all, a Soviet division at full strength was only two-thirds to three-quarters of the size of its Axis counterpart. Secondly, in all respects bar personal courage, the Soviet infantryman and his junior officers were not equal to the German. Thirdly, Soviet tactics were still stereotyped and wasteful. Fourthly, the Soviet armoured forces lacked the German experience of deep penetrations; *Blitzkrieg* was something they had read about in books, whereas the German commanders had been waging it successfully since 1939, and their familiarity with the hand-

ling and supplying of fast-moving tank and motorised infantry columns more than made up for their inferiority in quality of armour. As fighting vehicles, the German tanks – predominantly PzKw Marks III and IV – were markedly inferior to the heavy Russian KV-1, and especially to the medium T-34 (the most successful tank produced anywhere during the Second World War) in armour, gunpower, and mobility.

Moreover, Soviet inferiority had been increased by the débacle in the Barvenkovo salient in May which destroyed 29 Soviet infantry divisions and two-thirds of Timoshenko's tanks, leaving him outnumbered in armour by about 8 to 1 by the time the German attack began; and the German capture of the Crimea wiped out a further five Soviet armies with a total of at least fifteen divisions. Thus the relatively favourable balance of forces of early May had evaporated by the end of June, and the prognosis for a major German offensive in the south was good.

It would be tedious to try and trace the story of the manpower balance in detail throughout the battles which preceded those at Stalingrad itself; suffice it to say that when the Soviet Army Group entitled 'Stalingrad Front' was formed on July 12th, with 38 infantry divisions under command, 14 of those divisions had less than 1,000 men each and another six less than 4,000, against a full-strength establishment of 15,000. Three armies which had fought in the Kharkov offensive in May (21st, 28th, and 30th) had between them 21 divisions, all officially classified as 'remnants' and the 4th Tank Army formed on July 22nd, had 80 tanks; by August 10th it had none. There was no steam for the Russian steamroller here; and it was primarily the offensive out of the Barvenkovo salient which had brought the Red Army to this pitch.

'The Russian is finished'

On 28th June, Bock made his first move, launching IV Panzer Army against Voronezh, a key town in the Soviet lateral communications system behind the front line. Two days later he set VI Army in motion, heading north-eastwards against the same target with the aim of forming a pocket centred on Stary Oskol, in which the Soviet 6th, 21st, and 40th Armies would be trapped. The two German armies would be behind them, and the Hungarian II Army would be west of them. It would start the offensive off with a bang.

Timoshenko, however, refused to co-operate. Soviet sources do not say whether he had advance information, though he may well have had since on June 19th the operations officer of XXIII Panzer Division, Major Reichel, had made a forced landing close to the Russian lines while on a flight to a neighbouring corps headquarters. Reichel had with him some documents, including the objectives for phase one of 'Case Blue', which were not recovered and both his corps commander, General Stumme, and his divisional commander, General von

Boineburg-Lengsfeld, were relieved of their posts and later court-martialled for this breach of security.

It seems highly likely that the documents fell into Soviet hands, but whether the Soviet believed them or not is a different matter. 'Plants' of this kind are not unusual in war, and the mouths of many such gift horses were to be sceptically examined between 1939 and 1945. In any case, given the Soviet inferiority in forces on the southern sector of the front and Stavka's reluctance to move its reserve armies away from the central sector (it still believed at this point that the main German offensive would inevitably be aimed at Moscow) Timoshenko had no alternative but to withdraw, once the Panzer divisions were on the move. They were out to encircle and destroy his forces; once they had broken through, for him to stand fast was to play the game as they wanted him to.

But Voronezh had to be held, for if it fell, Soviet lateral communications would be imperilled; worse, the Germans would have the option of striking north behind Bryansk Front

towards Moscow. Stavka did not know that Moscow was definitely not on the German agenda for 1942, and the fact that Voronezh was the first German objective would reinforce the belief of those who considered the Reichel documents part of an elaborate deception. So Stavka reserves began to pour towards Voronezh; two 'combined-arms' (infantry) armies and one tank army took up positions on the east bank of the Don, while another tank army from the right wing of the adjacent Bryansk Front was redeployed to the area south of Yelets with orders to take IV Panzer Army in flank and rear. It was touch and go, for IV Panzer Army had already reached the Kastornoye – Stary Oskol railway by the evening of July 2nd, and put out a hook round the left flank of 40th Army, ready to gather it in, while VI Army, launched into battle on June 30th, was only 25 miles from Stary Oskol by nightfall on July 2nd, and was preparing to round up 21st and 28th Armies.

On this occasion, at least, Stavka reacted quickly. A new headquarters was hastily set up at Voronezh by Lieutenant-General F I Golikov and a group of staff officers to ensure on-the-spot control, and the Chief of the General Staff, Colonel-General A M Vasilevsky, flew at once from Moscow to Bryansk Front Headquarters. Everything was ready just in time. The Germans seized a bridgehead over the Don on July 6th, but against the entrenched Soviet forces were unable to make any progress, and while battering on the gates of Voronezh they found themselves in danger of being outflanked, when the Bryansk Front reserve launched its counter-attack from south of Yelets on the same day. The XXIV Panzer Corps and three infantry divisions had to be detached to cope with this new threat, and Voronezh was saved. To take it would now require a major operation.

This created the first major problem of decision for the German leadership. The stubbornness with which the Red Army defended Voronezh was due to Stavka's fear that its fall would be the prelude to a drive on Moscow, but since the Germans in fact had no intention of driving north, the quick capture of the city was secondary to the rounding up of Timoshenko's armies. And while the divisions of IV Panzer Army were engaged in the attempt to take the city – a task for which they were not suited, and which wasted their advantage of mobility – the armies of South-West Front were slipping quietly away behind strong rearguards, in good order, and with all their heavy equipment.

Hitler was not usually averse to taking his generals' decisions for them, but on this ocasion he showed unusual diffidence. On July 3rd he arrived at Bock's headquarters, but went no further than to say he 'no longer insisted' on the capture of Voronezh – but Bock was influenced by the fact that his patrols were already in the outskirts of the town, and persisted with the undertaking. As the Soviet reserves poured in, and a new Army Group (Voronezh Front) was set up, it became dangerous to relax the pressure for fear that the much increased Soviet forces would counterattack into the flank and rear of Bock's forces, and so much of IV Panzer Army was tied down there until July 13th; even then it failed to take the eastern part of the city, or to cut the Soviet supply lines north of the Don, and meanwhile Timoshenko's armies trudged away across the steppe, almost unmolested. Eventually Hitler lost patience, dismissed Bock, and thereafter blamed him for the failure of the offensive, as well as the disaster at Stalingrad in which it culminated six months later.

Even before Bock's dismissal, Hitler had intended to split Army Group South into two, one (A) to handle the thrust to the Caucasus, the other (B) to drive to the Volga; he now put this into effect, moved his headquarters from Rastenburg to Vinnitsa in the Ukraine, and embarked on a radical revision of the operational schedule, culminating in the issuing of Directive No. 45 on July 23rd. But before this Directive is considered, some account must be taken of the military situation, both as he saw it, and as it was in reality.

There is no doubt that the weakness of the Soviet resistance to the eastward advance of IV Panzer and V. Armies had surprised Hitler. His

THE OPENING MOVES

Armoured columns on the outer wheel . . .

motorised infantry inside

25

Top left: The easy advance . . . nowhere would the Russians stand and fight.
Bottom left: All the invaders saw of the enemy were the few unfortunate prisoners. *Above:* and the worthless trophies left behind by an army skilfully withdrawing

Command of the Armed Forces) claimed later that '. . . we were still waiting for a real great victory; it seemed to us that the enemy had still nowhere been brought to battle, as the small number of prisoners and the small amount of captured equipment proved.' He was right; but there is nothing to suggest that he or his superiors, except for Halder, waited other than in silence.

Admittedly, Hitler was always, until long after Stalingrad, reluctant to listen to suggestions that the Red Army was not at the end of its tether, and many months later, when his whole sleazy empire was falling about his ears, he ordered the head of 'Foreign Armies East' (the branch of Military Intelligence responsible for estimating the strength of the Red Army) to be committed to an asylum for estimates which the Führer regarded as exaggerated. So it probably required a stout heart, and contempt for one's career prospects, to suggest to the Supreme Warlord that the enemy was not yet breathing his last. Nevertheless, it seems odd that hardly any were sufficiently concerned to stand out against the euphoric vapourings of Hitler and his entourage. For the real situation was not quite so rosy.

Not that all was well with the Red Army. There was deep gloom among the Soviet public at the apparently endless retreat, and the 'spinelessness' of the men in the south, and their generals was being openly contrasted with the staunchness of the defenders of Leningrad and Moscow. This caused tensions between the southern generals and the men sent down from Stavka which persist to this day, for after all, if Timoshenko had been allowed to abandon his May offensive when he first requested permission, his forces would have been in a much better position to meet the German onslaught. Stavka and Stalin were the real villains of the piece, and the southern generals knew it; but the general public did not. All they knew, and all the common soldier knew, was that day by day more of the Soviet industrial heritage, built up so recently and at such sacrifices, was being surrendered to German predators.

troops were rolling ahead over the endless cornfields of the Ukraine at speeds reminiscent of the first heady weeks of the invasion in the previous summer, and the clouds of dust which marked their progress were hardly thicker than the fog of pseudo-sociological nonsense which the ideologists of Nazism were raising in premature exultation over the downfall of the Russian *Untermensch*. Even his generals, who sometimes tried to bring Hitler down to earth, seem to have fallen into the prevailing mood of euphoria. Halder, perhaps the most sceptical of them all, could find no answer, when Hitler said to him on July 20th 'The Russian is finished', other than 'I must admit, it looks like it'.

There was no denying that the Red Army was withdrawing in the south at speeds appropriate to panic flight, but their reluctance to stand and be encircled, and their refusal to abandon their heavy equipment, indicated a hasty but organised retreat to a more defensible line. General Warlimont, Deputy Chief of Operations Staff at Hitler's headquarters, OKW (High

The mood of the Soviet infantry as it trekked away into the big bend of the Don was thus one of depression and uncertainty, not relieved in the least by the exhortatory resolutions being passed by enthusiastic bodies of civilians deep in the rear. Morale was low, and many a Soviet officer has related how in those dark days of July his first task in the Stalingrad battle was to stand at a bridge or road junction, pistol in hand, organising stragglers into *ad hoc* units and listening to their ingenious reasons why they couldn't stop at the moment.

Nevertheless, the withdrawal was in general an orderly one, and its length was easily explained. The obvious place to stand and fight was at the eastern end of the big bend in the Don, and the timing of the withdrawal was governed by the rate at which the armies of the Stavka Reserve could be deployed to the south. These armies had, it will be recalled, been deployed in the centre so that they would be available to defend Moscow if necessary; they were all north of a line drawn from Borisoglebsk to Saratov, and did not begin to move south until early in July.

The sensible thing to do was to deploy them in the area of the Don bend, behind Timoshenko's retreating forces, and this was in fact what Stavka was doing with them. To have committed them piecemeal forward would no doubt have been more dramatic, but their installation in prepared positions made better military sense, though, of course, it also meant that they were not identified at the front, and this confirmed the Germans in their belief that the Red Army had no operational reserves left. The German actions that flowed from this misconception were to be catastrophic to the Wehrmacht, for so far from being finished, the Russians had 'not yet begun to fight'.

First, Hitler began to worry that the imminent collapse of the Red Army would necessitate dramatic action by the British and Americans, in the form of an invasion of Western Europe. He had denuded the West of twelve divisions during May and June, and transferred them to Russia for the summer offensive. Now he held back the élite SS Panzer Grenadier Division 'Leibstandarte Adolf Hitler' from the battle, and on July 9th ordered it to move to the West, later ordering the crack Motorised Infantry Division 'Gross Deutschland' to follow it. He then began to worry about possible Soviet diversionary action against Army Group Centre, and sent IX and XI Panzer Divisions to reinforce it.

On July 11th Hitler issued a Directive, No. 43, ordering Manstein's XI Army, fresh from the capture of Sebastopol, to cross the Kerch strait and take part in the invasion of the Caucasus, then a few days later, he countermanded it and despatched the entire army, except for one corps, away to the north, where its experience in capturing fortresses could be exploited for the capture of Leningrad (an operation which had survived from the first draft plan for a summer offensive where it made sense, to the final one where it did not, because the emphasis had been shifted to the south).

Then, to compound folly with folly, on July 13th, Hitler ordered IV Panzer Army, which was advancing on Stalingrad, to turn south-east and assist Kleist's I Panzer Army in seizing crossings over the lower Don east of Rostov. The IV Panzer had only just been released from its chore at Voronezh to resume the task allotted to it in the original Directive, but now it was diverted from that, to assist Kleist, whose forces (spearheading the southern arm of the pincer) had only been set in motion four days previously.

To make matters worse, Kleist did not need any help, for on that very day Stavka ordered a general withdrawal of South Front over the Don, except at Rostov, so that Hoth closed an almost empty bag and arrived at the Don crossings to find them almost undefended and the approach roads crowded with Kleist's traffic with which his own tanks then proceeded to entangle themselves, impeding Kleists' move into the Caucasus. After the war Kleist claimed that if IV Panzer had not been diverted in this way, it could have taken

Marshal S K Timoshenko

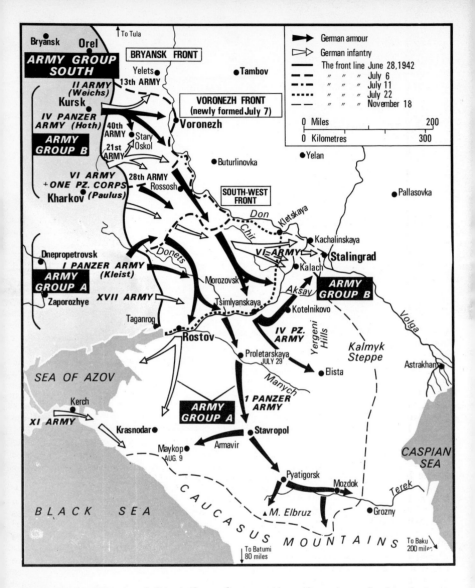

Stalingrad without a fight at the end of July. This is debatable, for Panzer divisions are not ideally suited to the taking of large cities, and substantial forces from Stavka reserve – notably 62nd and 64th Armies, already deploying in the area – would presumably have been switched to defend the city had it been under threat from a Panzer Army instead of from the overburdened infantry of VI Army.

But whatever the merits of Kleist's assertion, there is no doubt whatever that IV Panzer Army was not needed in Kleists' area, and at least one Soviet authority (Marshal Yeremenko) has gone so far as to describe its diversion as a 'gross strategic miscalculation'. Again, there is no evidence that any of the German generals objected at the time, whatever they may have said about it later, for they were unaware of the Stavka Directive for a general withdrawal, and hoped for a handsome

30

Col. General Hermann Hoth, commanding IV Panzer Army

tally of Soviet divisions – though so far they had had no luck. Even when the southern pincer (I Panzer and XVII Armies) had begun to move, it had done no more than shepherd South Front away before it, for just as South-West Front had hinged back on Veronozh, so South Front was hinging back on Rostov, and another attempt at encirclement had failed.

The High Command, however, still clung to the belief that the Red Army was finished, and it was at this point – July 23rd, 1942 – that Hitler issued his Directive No. 45. In view of the situation it was a surprising document. The orderly sequence of the original plan – first the Volga, then the Caucasus – was gone, and the two aims were to be achieved simultaneously. Nor was it now enough to be able to bombard Stalingrad – it must be taken. As for the Caucasus oilfields, Maikop and Grozny were not enough, despite the fact that the capture of Grozny would make it possible to cut off Soviet oil supplies by rail from the main fields at Baku. The main fields themselves must be taken, even though this would involve a crossing of the Caucasus Range – a major defen-

sive barrier with few passes and those at heights of over 10,000 feet, in narrow defiles where a few determined defenders could hold up an entire division.

The IV Panzer Army was still milling around at the Don crossings, and despite the need for it further north, it was six days before its orders were changed. On July 29th Hoth succeeded in putting his first tanks across the river; no sooner had he done so than he received new orders. He was to leave one division behind, to maintain contact with Kleist, and bring the rest back over the Aksay river to take Stalingrad from the south. The city had begun to seize the German imagination.

The Red Army had not been sitting back waiting for the Germans to make up their minds where to go next, for however the importance of Stalingrad might fluctuate in the minds of Hitler and his generals, there was no doubt of the place which it held in the Soviet mystique. The very name meant 'Stalin's city' – and names can be important. Had not Hitler changed the name of the pocket-battleship *Deutschland* because of the possible effects on morale if a ship named 'Germany' should be sunk? More than that, Stalin himself had played an important role in defeating the White armies of General Denikin at this place (then called Tsaritsyn) in 1920.

During the subsequent years, the city had been selected as a showpiece of the Soviet Union, and had become an industrial giant, stretching for twentyfive miles along the west bank of the Volga. Stalingrad sustained a population of 600,000 with its factories – three of which, the 'Red October' steel plant and 'Barricades' ordnance plant, and the Stalingrad Tractor Factory, stretched in a row along the river in the northern sector of the city and with their associated 'Workers' Settlements' immediately west of them, were to play an important part in the battle which was to come.

Though the city, as a special sign of Stalin's favour, was heavily laden with the wedding-cake architecture so dear to his heart, it was nevertheless a source of pride to its inhabitants, with parks and walks along the river bank, with numerous ravines and gullies running down to the Volga, and with many signs in its centre of the more spacious future to which all aspired. The Volga itself, almost a mile wide here had numerous islands in it; its west bank was high and steep, overhanging in places, and with many caves beneath the overhangs. Within the city were a number of low hills, one of which, the three hundred and thirty five foot high Mamayev Kurgan (Mamay's Burial Mound) commanded an excellent view of the city centre. Though there was no bridge over the Volga, there were important rail and road ferries, and the river port was an important one becoming even more so after the fall of Rostov and its rail routes on July 25th. This city would not be abandoned lightly by the Red Army.

A number of changes were now made in the organisation of defence of the area. South-West Front had been

Rostov. After its fall on July 25th, Stalingrad became even more vital to the Russian defence

abolished, and the Army Groups subordinated directly to Stavka, while the new Voronezh Front, formed to contain Bock on the north, had been put under a former Deputy Chief of General Staff, General N F Vatutin, while its neighbour to the north, Bryansk Front, came under another former Deputy CGS, General F I Golikov. These appointments both reflected the influence of Zhukov, for the two men had served under him in the recent past and both were to play prominent roles later in the

Stalingrad battle, as Zhukov's involvement in and direction of it increased. With South-West Front abolished, as its forces withdrew into the bend of the Don, they would be absorbed into the new Stalingrad Front which was being formed with troops of the Stavka reserve armies.

The new Front came officially into existence on July 12th, and Timoshenko at first commanded it, but it was clear that he would have to go – not into disgrace because on the whole the retreat into the Don

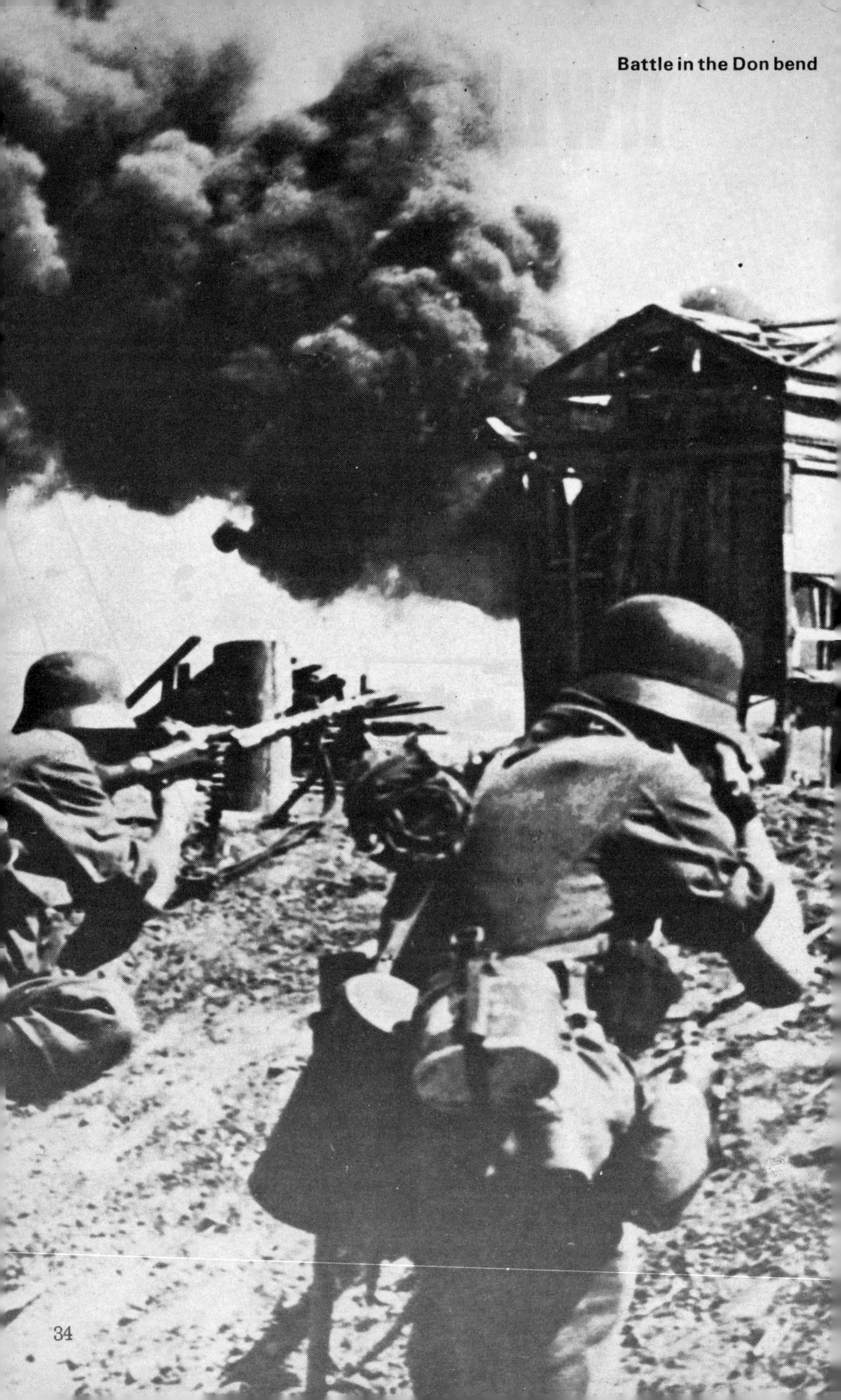

bend had been conducted with fair skill and economy, but because the new Front was too important to be commanded by a general around whom hung the smell of defeat; in any case he belonged to the older generation of Red Army commanders which was now yielding the field to men brought up in a more modern tradition, associated either with Zhukov himself, or with Zhukov's erstwhile patron, the great Marshal Tukhachevsky, whom Stalin had 'purged' and executed on a trumped-up charge of plotting with Germany against the Soviet state. So on July 22nd Timoshenko was given a senior command in the important but for the present less hectic north-western sector of the front, and his place was taken by General V N Gordov, who had just three days previously taken over command of 64th Army, one of the formations from Stavka reserve which had been deployed into the Don bend, and was in course of taking up its positions.

Army Group 'B' had formed three sub-groups for the attack on Stalingrad, and set them the following tasks: the Northern Group, consisting of two Panzer, two motorised, and four infantry divisions was to attack on July 23rd from the Golovsky-Perelazovsky area, aiming to capture the big bridge over the Don at Kalach, behind the Soviet forces deployed west of the Don. The central force, of one Panzer and two infantry divisions, attacking on July 25th, was to strike from the Oblivskaya – Verkhne-Aksenovsky area, also towards Kalach – and while these two groups formed a back-stop to the

Soviet forces in the Don bend, VI Army was to come in from the west and roll them up, thus leaving the road to the Volga open. The opportunity was then to be exploited by the third (southern) group, of one armoured, one motorised and four infantry divisions, which would have crossed the Don at Tsimlyanskay on the 21st and have established a large bridgehead from which it would advance on Stalingrad from the south, while the other two groups having finished their task in the Don bend, would advance to the Volga from west and north-west of the city.

For the execution of this plan the Commander-in-Chief of Army Group B, Colonel-General Freiherr von Weichs, had a total force equivalent to 30 divisions – though less than two-thirds of these were German – and over twelve hundred aircraft, outnumbering the Soviet forces in the Don bend by about two to one. For a defensive operation, however, this was not a hopelessly unfavourable ratio for the Soviet commanders. For them a much more serious disparity was that in weapons, as thanks largely to the losses in the Kharkov offensive, they were outnumbered by about two to one in tanks and guns, and three to one in aircraft, and to make matters worse nearly three hundred of the four hundred aircraft possessed by their 8th Air Army were of obsolete types, for the best of the newer aircraft – Yak-1 fighters, Pe-2 light bombers and the excellent Il-2 ground attack aircraft (the Sturmovik) – were available only in very small numbers. This meant in practice that the Germans had almost complete air superiority

Stormovik
Speed: 250 mph. Armament: 2 x 23mm cannon, 2 x 7.62 mg, 1 x 12.7 mg (rear).
Max Bomb load: 1,321 lbs bomb. Crew: 2

Stalingrad drew them on. *Below:* The panzers deploy. *Bottom:* German infantry columns fill the roads between Don and Volga

over the entire area.

Of his total of thirty divisions, Weichs was able to deploy about twenty against the Soviet forces in the Don bend (almost all of them German, and one of them Rumanian), to which he was able to add one more corps from early August, when Italian VIII Army began arriving to take over its sector along the Don each side of Veshenskaya. The Soviet forces comprised the 62nd and 64th Armies, supported by 1st Tank Army (which had one hundred and sixty tanks) and 4th Tank Army (which had eighty tanks), while in the northern corner of the bend was 1st Guards Army, which played no particular part in the battle except to hold a bridgehead south of the river at Kremenskaya. But all the armies which had to take the main weight of the German attack were newly formed, and the two tank armies were particularly raw, as they came into existence only on July 22nd.

Apart from some skirmishing between XIV Panzer Corps and the forward elements of 62nd Army along the River Chir from July 17th onwards, there was no major action until July 23rd, when five German divisions attacked the right wing of 62nd Army north of Manoylin, while 64th Army found itself under attack on the river Tsimla. After three days of fighting, XIV Panzer Corps broke through 62nd Army's defences and advanced to Kamensky on the Don, outflanking 62nd Army from the north. The 1st Tank Army, which was deployed behind 62nd, attempted to cut off the German force by attacking due north across its rear, while 4th Tank Army tried a heading-off attack from the north of the German salient – but as neither army had been in existence for more than five days, as both contained a heterogenous mixture of tanks and non-motorised infantry, were still only partially equipped and were commanded by infantry officers who lacked experience of working with armour, it was hardly likely their attacks would succeed; and they did not – especially as they were not co-ordinated in any way, and were given weak artillery support and practically no air cover.

While this mismanaged attack was

37

faltering to its inevitable end, XXIV Panzer Corps was driving a wedge between 62nd and 64th Armies as it headed for Kalach from the south-west along the west bank of the Don. Stavka became very uneasy at the southern penetration and on July 28th ordered Gordov to strengthen the southern defences of the area between the rivers from Logovsky on the Don to Raygorod on the Volga, so on August 1st he deployed 57th Army and some of his reserve units along the line in question, and was also given command of 51st Army, which was to be deployed south of the Volga bend from the Sarpa Lakes to the point where the front line petered out in the Kalmyk Steppe towards Rostov. This gave Stalingrad Front a total front line nearly four hundred and forty miles long, and in view of the difficulty of administering such a long front, it was decided to establish a new Army Group, South-East Front, which would take over the southern half of Gordov's line. The search for a suitable officer to command it began at once.

Meanwhile the situation at the front in the Don bend had quietened down to some extent, as although the German mobile forces had reached the Don and made deep penetrations on each side of 62nd Army, the untried troops from Stavka reserve had acquitted themselves well, and neither VI nor IV Panzer Armies was in any position to force the Don line, or round up 62nd Army, without pausing to regroup. Most of IV Panzer had by now come back from its useless expedition to the Don crossings in the south, and on July 31st Hoth took it on to the offensive in the Tsimlyanskaya area against the over-extended 51st Army, which with five understrength infantry divisions was attempting to cover a one hundred and twenty five mile front from Verkhne-Kurmoyarskaya to Orlovskaya.

Hoth's blow broke through 51st Army's defences, and it began a hasty withdrawal towards the Tikhoretsk – Krasnoarmeysk railway; and so by August 2nd he had reached Kotelnikovo, and there remained between him and Stalingrad only eighty four miles of country with some minor natural obstacles, the chief of which were the Aksay and Myshkova rivers.

There had been some command changes in Stalingrad Front; 62nd Army had been taken over by General A I Lopatin, while the acting commander of 64th Army, Lieutenant-General A I Chuykov, had handed his army over to Major-General M S Shumilov, returned to report to Front headquarters in Stalingrad, quarrelled with Gordov (for whose qualities as a Front commander he had little respect) and returned to 64th Army to give a written account of the withdrawal of some of the army's units across the Chir while under his command. On the morning of August 2nd, Shumilov sent for him, told him of Hoth's breakthrough which threatened

to outflank the entire army and maybe the entire front, and suggested he go to the southern sector to take charge.

Chuykov was only too pleased to get out of writing the report for Gordov, and left at once. On arrival in the southern sector, he discovered two Soviet infantry divisions, part of 51st Army, wandering across the steppe on their way to Stalingrad to rejoin the army with which they had lost contact, taking with them two regiments of *Katyusha* rocket mortars, obviously shaken by the heavy losses they had suffered from Hoth's attack, but with no radio. Chuykov commandeered them, positioned them behind the Aksay river and put a brigade of marines behind them to stiffen their resolution. He then contacted Front HQ, reported what he had done and was told that 208th Infantry Division from Siberia was detraining in the area and should also come under his command – if he could find its HQ whose whereabouts were unknown.

After several hours' searching he found that the division had begun to detrain on the previous day, but that four trainloads had been shot up by German aircraft and the survivors scattered. A little further on, at Chilekov station, he found several more trainloads of troops of the division detraining, but suddenly

Russian rolling stock . . . shot up, the reinforcements scattered

twenty seven German aircraft appeared and bombed the station, causing heavy casualties among the troops, and putting his radio out of action. Cursing Gordov for not having ensured air cover for the division, Chuykov went on rounding up stragglers, organising them into units and sending them off on assignments.

With this improvised force he organised a defence along the Aksay, sent out reconnaissance patrols which

established that Hoth's main force was making a wide detour to the east – obviously with intention of striking at Stalingrad from the south. Chuykov's own force on the Aksay was attacked on August 6th but drove the German and Rumanian infantry back, and in fact held on to its positions until ordered to pull back on August 17th in conformity with a general withdrawal of the entire line. He had learned some useful lessons in breaking up German attacks, and was to put them to good use in a more important role at several crucial stages later in the battle.

On the main front in the Don bend, the situation for the Red Army had worsened following the failure of the counterattack. The 62nd Army had lost most of its eight infantry divisions, which fought their way out in small groups but left much of their equipment behind and would take some time to re-assemble and re-equip. In their place, it had gained some of the divisions of 1st Tank Army which had been disbanded, as well as one division which belonged to 64th Army but had been levered away to the north by the German penetration between the two armies. The great bridge at Kalach had been seized intact by a daring *coup de main* of a small body of German assault engineers, and the German tanks could begin crossing into the neck of land between Don and Volga. Gordov had made a bad start as a Front commander, and clearly could not hold the position much longer.

By August 16th the last bridgehead on the stretch of the Don which runs from north to south between Kamensky and Verkhne-Kurmoyarskaya had been given up, but further north, along the west-east stretch of the Don before it reaches the big bend, 1st Guards and 21st Armies remained in possession of several stretches of the south bank between Kletskaya and Serafimovich, and were even to extend them, while the Rumanians of III Army remained stolidly on the defensive. These forgotten bridgeheads, about which no-one at OKW, OKH, or Army Group B then seemed concerned, were to prove decisive when the heat and dust of August had given place to the snows of November.

Yeremenko takes over

At first, Stalin was concerned to find not a replacement for Gordov, but a commander for the new South-East Front, but in view of subsequent developments, caused by Gordov's unsatisfactory handling of the battle in the Don bend, more than ordinary significance was to attach to the appointment of the man given charge of the new Army Group.

On August 1st a thick-set Soviet general was arguing with his doctor in a room of a hospital in Moscow, where he was recovering from a leg injury, his second serious wound of the war. He was attempting to persuade the doctor that he was fit to return to duty, and after some acrimonious discussion about the rights of patients versus doctors in deciding when a man was fit to leave, the irate doctor had subjected him to a practical test of his ability to walk without his stick. Half a dozen steps brought out a cold sweat on his forehead, and his leg went numb.

'Enough, enough,' cried the doctor triumphantly. 'Now it is clear, esteemed Colonel-General, who is mistaken about the moment of re-covery. There's still fundamental healing to be done'.

Sheepishly the general confessed that he had already reported himself to Stavka as ready to return to the front.

'So much the worse for you', said the doctor, 'Without a note from the doctor in charge they won't even look at your report.'

Bluff having failed, the general resorted to an emotional appeal. 'Tell me, Professor, hand on heart, if you were suffering from an illness like mine, in its present stage, could you sit calmly on one side, knowing that hundreds of people were dying from wounds and waiting for your help, yours, Professor, no-one else's?'

The professor thought about this, but gave no direct answer. In the end he said 'All right then, if you give me your word of honour to follow strictly the régime I prescribe, I won't object to your discharge.'

The general spent the rest of the day practising walking without a stick, while he waited for a telephone call. Towards midnight it came, from the Secretary to the People's Commissar for Defence. 'Your report has been examined. Come to the Kremlin at once.'

He left his stick in Stalin's outer office, and walked carefully but boldly into the meeting room of the State Defence Committee. Stalin, who was just concluding a telephone call, turned to him, looked him carefully in the eye and said, 'Well, so you think you're all right?'

'Yes, I've recovered,' said the general.

One of the other members of the committee remarked on his limp, but he passed it off with an assurance of well-being which he was far from feeling.

'Well then,' said Stalin, 'we'll consider you as back in the ranks. You're very necessary to us just now. Let's get down to business. At Stalingrad now circumstances have so turned out that we can't get by without taking steps to strengthen this very important sector of the front, and without steps calculated to improve the direction of the troops. It has been decided to divide the Stalingrad Front which was formed recently into two. The State Defence Committee intends to assign you to head one of them. What's your view on it?'

'I am ready to serve anywhere you think it necessary to send me' answered the general. His name was Andrey Ivanovich Yeremenko, his rank, Colonel-General, and his age thirty-nine.

Yeremenko was one of Stalin's favourite trouble-shooters, and had already received some difficult assignments, not all of which had been successfully carried out. But he was strategically gifted, and a fire-eating optimist who thrived on challenges. Perhaps his optimism sometimes ran away with him, and perhaps he was rather prone to cast himself as a man of destiny, but the situation was not one for the faint-hearted, and no-one had ever accused him of being that. He at once departed for the General Staff building to familiarise himself with the situation in the south, and returned to Stalin's office that evening. After some argument with Stalin about the desirability of maintaining a single Front in the area (implicitly with himself in charge of it instead of Gordov), he bowed to Stalin's decision, and then asked for the command of the northern of the two Fronts, pointing out that the long German flank along the Don would be very vulnerable to a counterattack, which was more suited to his temperament than defence. Stalin heard him out, and replied 'Your proposal deserves attention, but that's a matter for the future; at present we have to stop the German offensive'.

He paused to fill his pipe, and Yeremenko hastened to agree with him.

'You understand correctly', resumed Stalin, 'and that is why we are sending you to South-East Front, to hold up and stop the enemy who is striking from the Kotelnikovo area towards Stalingrad. South-East Front must be created from scratch, and quickly. You have experience of this; you set up Bryansk Front from scratch [in 1941]. So go, rather, fly, tomorrow to Stalingrad and set up South-East Front'.

Yeremenko arrived in Stalingrad on the morning of August 4th, and was met at the airfield by a car sent by his 'Member of Military Council', the man responsible for overseeing the Political Department of the Front, responsible for indoctrination, propaganda, morale, and welfare of the troops, for ensuring the maximum co-operation from the local Party authorities, for obtaining co-operation from the Party and Government in Moscow, if need be, and (discreetly) for ensuring that Yeremenko remained 'politically' sound. The 'Member of Military Council' was no stranger to the south; he was the First Secretary of the Ukrainian Communist Party, and had served Timoshenko in the capacity which he now fulfilled with Yeremenko. His rank as a Commissar was equivalent to a Lieutenant-General, and he was a short, very stocky man with an earthy ebullience which after the war would become known to the world at large. His name was Nikita Sergeyevich Khruschchev.

Yeremenko was given four days to set up the South-East Front, and was to enter into command on August 9th. The line dividing his responsibilities from those of Gordov ran straight

41

Above: Col. Andrey Invanovich Yeremenko. *Below:* His Political Commisar Lieutenant-General Nikita Sergeyevich Khruschev

PZKW III
These would spearhead the attack. Weight: 25.4 tons. Speed: 28 mph. Armour (max): 50mm. Crew: 5. Armament: 1 x 50mm. 2 x 7.92mm mg

76.2 mm. These would keep it at bay. *Weight:* 3,500 lbs. *Range:* (ceiling) 14,766 yds. *Ammunition:* 13.75 lb shell

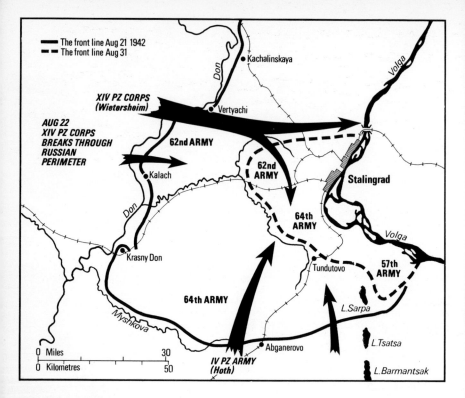

The front line Aug 21 1942
The front line Aug 31

XIV PZ CORPS (Wietersheim)

AUG 22 XIV PZ CORPS BREAKS THROUGH RUSSIAN PERIMETER

Kachalinskaya

Don

Volga

Vertyachi

62nd ARMY

62nd ARMY

Kalach

Stalingrad

64th ARMY

Don

Volga

Krasny Don

Tundutovo

57th ARMY

64th ARMY

L.Sarpa

Myshkova

L.Tsatsa

Abganerovo

0 Miles 30

0 Kilometres 50

IV PZ ARMY (Hoth)

L.Barmantsak

across from Kalach and down the valley of the Tsaritsa river to the Volga, thus cutting the city area into two. His headquarters were in an underground installation, the Tsaritsyn Bunker, which had been specially built earlier in the year. No sooner had he begun to organise his headquarters than his reactions were put to the test, as on August 7th, Hoth's Panzers (which Chuykov had observed by-passing the Aksay line on the 5th and 6th) approached Stalingrad from the south, drove in 64th Army's left flank, and came within nineteen miles of the city. He could expect no help from Stalingrad Front, whose forces were fully committed, and his other armies (51st and 57th) were much below strength, 51st having only the equivalent of one full-strength division in the area – the remnants of two others were still on the Aksay line with Chuykov, too far away to be of assistance.

Panic broke out in the city, and draconian measures had to be taken to keep civilians off the roads needed for military traffic, after which an improvised force of tanks, anti-tank guns, and *Katyusha* rocket mortars was hastily assembled and sent down to confront Hoth at Abganerovo. Several days of fierce fighting followed the first clash on August 9th, but eventually Hoth's penetration was stopped, and he abandoned for the moment the attempt to break through from the south. Thus Yeremenko had passed his first test, but sterner ones were to come, beginning on August 10th, while the fighting at Abganerovo was at its height.

On that day a very serious situation arose on the left wing of Stalingrad Front, immediately adjacent to Yeremenko's right, when General Lopatin's 62nd Army got into difficulties while attempting a counterattack with three of its divisions. Although they caused the Germans some losses they themselves became surrounded on three sides, and were able to escape only with great difficulty and heavy casualties, and though the German advance stopped for the time being on

44

Rocket Artillery. Katyusha rocket mortar batteries helped to stem the first onslaught at Abganerovo. They fired in salvoes

the west bank of the Don, the situation remained critical because the natural line of advance towards Stalingrad was directly athwart the line of demarcation between Stalingrad and South-East Fronts, with all the difficulties entailed in coordinating operations between two commanders of equal status, especially as concerned the movement of reserves, of which Yeremenko at that time had none, thus being forced to rely on Gordov (whom almost every Soviet senior officer seems to have found most difficult to work with or for, and who at that time had none either). Yeremenko reported the difficulty to Stavka, with the perhaps unexpected result that late on the evening of the 13th he found himself appointed to command both Fronts, with Gordov as his Deputy for Stalingrad Front and Golikov (late of Bryansk Front) fulfilling the same duties in respect of South-East Front. Thus he became the Supreme Commander on the spot, and though members of Stavka frequently visited his HQ, any decisions which had to be taken quickly, were taken by him. His faculty for snap action was soon to be tested to the full, for Paulus was about to mount the most serious threat so far, in the form of an attack on the city from north, west and south.

Hitler had been rather restive about the failure of his generals to capture Stalingrad. and Paulus was nothing if not responsive to his master's wishes. The deadline of August 25th had been set for the capture of the city, and this was now getting near, so operational orders for the capture of the city were issued by VI Army HQ on August 19th, and the start of the operation was set for 0430 hours on the 23rd. In the first phase a mobile spearhead composed of XVI Panzer, III and 60th Motorised Divisions, commanded by Lieutenant-General Hube, would blast a path across the corridor between Don and Volga from bridgeheads either side of Vertyachi. When they had reached the northern suburbs of Stalingrad (Spartakovka, Rynok and Latashinka), they would prepare to move south into the city, while follow-up forces consolidated and widened the corridor seized by them. The IV Panzer Army would then blast into the city from the south, once it had been sealed off on its northern side, and General von Seydlitz-Kurzbach's 51st. Corps would head east from Kalach, maintaining contact on its north flank with the follow-up to Hube's force and aiming to hit Stalingrad at the junction between 62nd and 64th Armies so as to cut them off from each other.

At the appointed hour Hube's force set off, overrunning the Soviet defences by weight, speed, and efficiency. Miles away to the south-east they could see the clouds of smoke raised as Stalingrad burned under the attacks of Luftflotte IV, which that day flew over 2,000 sorties in a terror

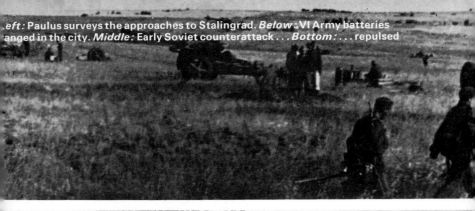
Left: Paulus surveys the approaches to Stalingrad. *Below:* VI Army batteries anged in the city. *Middle:* Early Soviet counterattack . . . *Bottom:* . . . repulsed

1

5

48

PREPARATION FOR BATTLE

1 Anti-tank guns move up
2. Mobile light artillery screens deploy
3. The Luftwaffe harries the defenders
4. Signallers lay the lines
5. The inevitable 88s . . .
6. . . . and the indefatigable panzers

The opening barrage. *Bottom:* **The first prisoners**

campaign familiar to those at Warsaw and Rotterdam. By mid-afternoon Hube's men were in sight of the city itself, and as the evening drew in they smashed their way through the improvised defence put up by the women workers of the 'Barricades' Factory manning anti-aircraft guns, and rolled on to the high western bank of the Volga north of Rynok. There they spent the night preparing for the next day's battle, in which surely the city would fall. But unknown to them, Yeremenko was about to perform an act of midwifery, bringing a fortress to birth out of a dead city.

He had awakened early that morning, to the news that the Germans were on the move at the junction between 62nd and 4th Tank Armies (4th Tank now had only infantry; all its tanks had been lost in the battle in the Don bend); so at dawn he alerted Colonel Sarayev, the commander of 10th Division of troops of the NKVD (People's Commissariat for Internal Affairs). These were essentially internal security troops, the uniformed cousins of the secret police, and thus had no heavy weapons such as artillery – but in spite of this, the defence of the thirty-one mile long city defence perimeter was in their hands, as the regular army formations could not be spared for the task.

At 0800 hours, Yeremenko rang HQ 62nd Army for a situation report, from which it became clear that the Germans were heading straight for the city at high speed. At 0900, the Chief of Staff of 8th Air Army, General Seleznev, rang. 'Pilots just back from reconnaissance report heavy fighting in the Malaya Rossoshka area. Everything on the ground's burning. The pilots saw two columns of about 100 tanks each, followed by dense columns of infantry in trucks. It's all moving towards Stalingrad. The heads of the columns are passing the Malaya Rossoshka line. Large groups of enemy aircraft are bombing our forces to clear the way for their columns.'

Yeremenko wasted no words. 'My decision: put up all aircraft of Stalingrad Front at once. Strike a powerful blow at the columns of enemy tanks and motorised infantry'. He then telephoned Major-General of Air Forces TT Khryukin, commanding the air forces of South-East Front, ordering him to commit all his ground attack aircraft against Hube's column, after which he summoned his chief of armour, General Shtevnev, and Head of Operations, General Rukhle.

The telephone rang again. It was Khrushchev. 'What's new?'

'Not specially pleasant news.'

'I'll come to HQ at once.'

And again, this time the commander of the anti-aircraft corps, Colonel Raynin, reporting that his sound detectors at Bolshaya Rossoshka had picked up the noise of Hube's tanks. Yeremenko ordered him to be ready to use his guns against tanks and aircraft, as the city was bound to be bombed soon.

Now Shtevnev and Rukhle had arrived, so he ordered Shtevnev to scrape together the remnants of two tank corps about to be sent to the rear to re-form and re-equip, to block the German advance and prepare for a counterattack (a forlorn hope, this, considering that . the two corps had between them fewer than 50 tanks, most of them the obsolete T-70). Rukhle was sent off to prepare the appropriate orders.

It was now 1100 hours and Khrushchev had arrived to report that the Party organisations and the workers' formations were prepared to join in the defence, and wanted to be given assignments. An air of uneasiness pervaded the headquarters, and it required an effort of will on Yeremenko's part to maintain a facade of calmness among all the frenzied activity. The phone rang again. The Head of Communications, Major-General Korshunov reported in a worried tone that a trainload of ammunition, food and reinforcements had been shot up by the German armour.

'The enemy tanks are moving on Stalingrad. What are we to do?' 'Your duty. Stop panicking.' replied Yeremenko sharply.

Colonel Sarayev, of the NKVD, came in.

'The enemy tanks are nine to ten miles from Stalingrad, and moving fast towards the northern part of the city,' said Yeremenko.

'I know,' said Sarayev in a whisper.

'What have you done?'

'In accordance with your previous orders I have told the two regiments occupying the defences on the north and north-west to be ready for battle.'

Yeremenko ordered that in addition the reserve regiment in Minina suburb should redeploy to the 'Barricades' factory in the threatened area.

Now his Deputy for South-East Front, Lieutenant-General Golikov, was on the line. The plot was thickening. The IV Panzer Army had begun attacking from the south at 0700; by noon they had captured Tinguta station and the siding at the seventy-four kilometre marker. The 38th Rifle Division was partially surrounded, but elsewhere the Germans had been beaten off, and a counter attack on Tinguta was being prepared. 'Good, carry on. Order 56th Tank Brigade in

South-East Front reserve to prepare for immediate action.'

Food was brought in, but there was no time to eat. The Deputy Chief of General Staff was on the line from Moscow, wanting to know how the situation was developing. While Yeremenko was talking to him, word was brought that the commander of 62nd Army, General Lopatin, wanted to speak at once on the telephone.

'Lopatin reporting. Up to 250 tanks and about 1,000 truckloads of motorised infantry with very strong simultaneous air support have wiped out a regiment of 87th Rifle Division and the right flank of 35th Guards Rifle Division north of Malaya Rossoshka.'

'I know. Take steps to close the breach at once and throw the enemy back from the middle perimeter, restore the situation.'

Now Colonel Raynin reported that his guns were fighting tanks east of Orlovka, and had suffered some losses, and Colonel Sarayev came to say that the 282nd Regiment of 10th NKVD Division was engaged with enemy tanks and motorised infantry east of Orlovka. Yeremenko began to run over in his mind the state of his reserves; he had some specially good units which had already proved themselves, but they were not many – one brigade of tanks, one of motorised infantry, rather more than one of tank-destroyers, and one infantry brigade now on its way. The telephone rang to interrupt his chain of thought This time not a soldier, but Malyshev, the Minister for Tank Production and representative of the State Defence Committee, speaking from the Stalingrad Tractor Factory, which had become a major producer of tanks.

'From the factory we can see fighting going on north of the city. AA gunners fighting tanks [these were the guns manned by women factory workers which Hube's column overran in late afternoon]. Several shells have already fallen in the factory area. The enemy tanks are advancing on Rynok. We've prepared the most important targets for blowing up.'

'Don't blow anything up yet. Defend the factory at whatever cost. Get the workers' detachment ready for battle and keep the enemy out of the factory. Help is already on its way.'

Malyshev handed the phone over to Major-General Feklenko. 'I'm at the tank training centre, I have about 2,000 men and 30 tanks. I have decided to defend the factory.'

'A correct decision. I appoint you sector commander. Organise the defence of the factory with forces of the training centre and workers' detachment at once. Two brigades are on their way to you, one tank, one rifle.'

Now the Chief Engineer of South-East Front, accompanied by its supply officer, arrived, to report proudly that they had completed the building of a pontoon bridge across the Volga from the Tractor Factory in ten days, two days less than scheduled. The bridge was nearly two miles long.

'Very good. Thank the men who built it and the officers who supervised them, especially Comrade Stepanov and the others. As for the bridge, I order it to be destroyed.'

The two technical men looked at each other, wondering whether Yeremenko had gone off his head.

'Yes, yes, destroy it, and immediately.' He explained briefly why it had to be done, and they left to do his bidding.

At they left, the artillery specialists, Major-Generals Degtyarev and Zubanov came to report that the Germans were very close to the main ammunition stores, and were told to shift as much of the ammunition as possible to a safe place.

Now came some better news. Colonel Gorokhov entered to report the arrival of his troops, 124th Rifle Brigade, on the opposite bank. 'Get your brigade over as fast as you can and take it to the Tractor Factory. Report to Comrade Feklenko there; he'll give you your assignment.'

Again Yeremenko tried to eat his breakfast (it was now nearly 1800 hours) but again the telephone rang. Colonel Raynin reported 'Large groups of German bombers approaching Stalingrad from west and southwest. They'll be over the city in three to five minutes. The air raid alarm has been sounded, the combat order has been given, and the fighters are taking off.'

'Right. Carry on', said Yeremenko, as calmly as he could, while his heart began to beat fast; and sweat broke out on his forehead. 'Big groups' – that meant thirty or forty in each group; at least one hundred aircraft (in fact it was about six times that, since many of the aircraft made several sorties). As the aircraft came in Hube's force began to attack southward from Rynok. First they were met by mortar and anti-aircraft gun fire; soon the tank-destroyer battalions with anti-tank rifles came up, and hastily took up a position on the Sukhaya Mechetka creek, half a mile north of the Tractor Factory, After some hours of hard fighting Hube's tanks retired to refuel, repair and take on ammunition for the next day. While they did so, the hard-pressed defenders of the Tractor Factory were being reinforced.

At last Yeremenko could have his breakfast.

Death of a city

The fires started by the German bombers burned through the night, and the sun rose next morning on a scene of utter devastation. There had been two months of sunny weather without any rain, and the houses in the suburbs, predominantly of wood, had gone up like tinder, so that over huge areas of the outskirts only the brick chimney-stacks remained, like so many tombstones. In the centre and the industrial area, where the buildings were of more substantial construction, things looked at first sight more normal, but closer inspection revealed that inside the walls were nothing but charred heaps of ruins. Some oil storage tanks had gone up like gigantic fireworks, releasing their contents to flow in burning streams down to the Volga, there to spread, still burning, over its surface. The jetties had gone up in flames, as had many of the ships there. The telephone system had ceased to function, as the wooden telephone poles had flared up and gone, and the very asphalt of the roadways had added its measure to the holocaust. Early bombing had put the water system out of action, so that the firemen could but watch helplessly as the streams of water from their hoses dwindled first to a trickle and then to nothing.

Because of the nearness of their airfields, the bombers were able to make several trips each, and during the day Stalingrad had received the equivalent of two thousand-bomber raids. By the morning of the 24th the city was in ruins, and thousands of its citizens lay dead. Though after the war many German authors were to claim that the raids had pursued strictly military objectives, it had been primarily a terror raid. True, the blocking of roads by fallen buildings hampered the movement of Yeremenko's forces to the threatened sectors of the front line, and true, there was always the chance that the Command Post would be put out of action; but there were few Soviet troops in the actual city area, as most of them were deployed outside it in the outer and middle defence perimeters.

Later experience of the Western Allies at Cassino and Caen was to show that destruction of large build-ings can assist a determined defender by impeding the attackers' access to his positions and to that extent, the German bombing of Stalingrad was a mistake. The exercise of hindsight is one of the more pernicious vices of the historian, but it is tempting to wonder what the outcome would have been if Luftflotte IV had been enough of a precision instrument to be used instead against the static troops of the 10th NKVD Division, Feklenko's men in the grounds of the Tractor Factory, or Golikov's tanks assembling to counterattack at Tinguta. For the fact was that when on the morning of the 24th the Germans renewed their attack on the ground, they ran into a defence of rock-like consistency, and it was this sudden elusiveness of a prize which had seemed within their grasp which led them from then on to apply more and more force at the tip of a long and vulnerable penetration, in complete disregard of the danger to which their northern flank along the Don was exposed.

Nor was there any vital necessity to do so, as on August 23rd Hube's men had in fact attained the aims set out in the original plan – to establish a line from Don to Volga at the point where they were nearest to each other, and to bring Stalingrad and the Volga under fire. In addition, they had split Stalingrad Front in two, and cut the railway lines on which its lateral communications were heavily dependent. Yet the German corridor across the neck of land between Volga and Don was still very narrow, and Yeremenko hoped to snip through it so as to restore the integrity of his front. When the tanks and motorised infantry of Hube's columns attacked along the Sukhaya Mechetka on the morning of the 24th, they met with such heavy opposition from Feklenko's mixed bag of reinforcements – ranging from Gorokhov's infantry brigade to battalions of Stalingrad militia – that so far from gaining ground, they made no progress all morning, were counterattacked in the late afternoon, and forced back one and a quarter miles.

Meanwhile, the bombers continued to make most of their attacks not on the Soviet positions in the vital northern sector, but on the city area

itself. This did not make Yeremenko's
and Khrushchev's task any easier, as
urgent arrangements had to be made
to evacuate women, children, and old
people across the Volga, and the signs
of disorder and confusion among the
civilian population forced Yeremenko
to declare martial law on the 25th; but
every bomb that fell on the city was
one bomb less on Feklenko's force
north of the Tractor Factory, and his
men made full use of the relief thus
afforded.

Balked on the north, VI Army now
attempted to break in from the west.
Under cover of the morning mists on
August 25th, a group of 25 tanks and
an infantry division crossed the Don
south of Rubezhnoye and began to
advance on the central part of Stalingrad. They were halted by a combat
group of one tank brigade (169th) and
one infantry division (35th Guards)
under the command of Yeremenko's
deputy for Stalingrad Front, Major-
General Kovalenko. The combat group
fought its way into the partially
encircled 87th Rifle Division at Bol-

shaya Rossoshka, and relieved it. A
group of 33 soldiers of 87th Rifle Division, all from Siberia and the Far East,
like so many of Russia's best soldiers,
performed a remarkable exploit in
holding out for two days against a
force of 70 German tanks which had
surrounded them, and destroying 27 of
them, making especially good use of
the improvised weapon known to the
whole world as a 'Molotov cocktail',
but (because of its unfortunate asso-
ciations with the Soviet invasion of
Finland in 1939) described more pro-
saically by Soviet authors as 'a
bottle with an inflammable mixture'.
Despite the fact that most of them had
never seen action before, their total
casualties were one man wounded,
and though this was by no means
typical of Soviet operations, in which
casualties were often unnecessarily
heavy because of the primitive nature
of small-unit tactics, it was a pointer
to the way in which the battle in the
city itself should be fought.

With the Germans for the moment
fended off at the outskirts of the city,

The onslaught: Terror attack launched against the city area. *Bottom:* The bombardment closes in

Yeremenko's thoughts turned to the
counterattack for which he was so
eager. His object was to force XIV
Panzer Corps to abandon its corridor
through to the Volga, or, hopefully, to
destroy it, and the means by which
he hoped to achieve this was by getting
astride its lines of communication,
using the 21st and 1st Guards Armies
in the north (a Soviet 'Guards' formation was one which had distinguished
itself in battle. It received a better
scale of equipment, and its men were
given higher pay; it was not, however,
formed from specially selected re-
cruits like 'Guards' units in other
armies).

On the 24th, two divisions of 21st
Army had already begun to probe the
German positions at Serafimovich and
Kletskaya, and part of 1st Guards had
attacked near Novo-Grigoryevskaya;
it extended its bridgehead on the right
bank of the Don, but the forces employed were not strong enough to cut
off Hube's force. On the 25th several
divisions of 63rd Army attacked from
the Yelanskaya-Zimovsky line, moving south and capturing another
bridgehead across the Don. General
Kovalenko's combat group had by now
been reinforced by two more rifle
divisions and some tanks, and on the
26th it put in another counterattack
out of the Samofalovka area in an
effort to lever the Germans off a number of commanding heights, but there
was not enough artillery support, the
attack was badly co-ordinated, and
the Luftwaffe too strong, so the attack
was a complete failure.

Now General Shtevnev put in an
attack in the neighborhood of Gorodishche and Gumrak, with a force
drawn from 62nd Army. This succeeded in blocking for the time being any
further attempts at a break-in from
north-west of the city, but again was
not strong enough to achieve any
more than that, so Yeremenko's
cherished project of an attack down
on the northern flank of VI Army had
to be abandoned for lack of forces.
How near it had come to success,
Yeremenko was not to know until

Top: Luftwaffe troops move up through
outlying villages
Bottom: Armoured car on the banks of
the Volga

after the war, when it became known that the C-in-C XIV Panzer Corps, General von Wietersheim, had become so uneasy about the fate of Hube's column , isolated on the bank of the Volga, and at times dependent solely on air drops for supply, that he decided to withdraw it, only to be overruled by the C-in-C of Army Group 'B', Colonel-General von Weichs.

Now, however, a new threat arose on the southern sector. The IV Panzer Army had been trying since August 19th to break through the southern corner of the Stalingrad defences at Tundutovo, but with no success to speak of and very heavy casualties, especially to its XXIV Panzer Division, as the Soviet defences on the high ground between Beketovka and Krasnoarmeysk on the Volga were elaborate, well-designed, and manned by several divisions of the Soviet 64th Army with tank support. Hoth had therefore called off the attack, and while Yeremenko was heavily occupied with making counterattacks north and north-west of Stalingrad, IV Panzer Army's tanks and motorised infantry were being quietly moved round from the southern to the southwestern sector to regroup at Abganerovo, whence they were launched at dawn on the 29th against 126th Rifle Division of 64th Army. Hoth's intention was to hammer a wedge into the centre of 64th Army, then to execute a right-turn into the rear of the Soviet positions between Beketovka and Krasnoarmeysk, thus by-passing the strongpoints which he had been trying in vain to reduce by frontal assaults, capturing the Volga bank and high ground south of Stalingrad, and cutting off the left wing of 64th Army.

However, the German attack went better than expected. General von Hauenschild's XXIV Panzer Divison broke through the Soviet line at Gavrilovka with the aid of some very effective work by the 'Stuka' dive-bombers of Luftflotte IV, and penetrated into the rear areas of both 62nd and 64th Armies. At once the situation changed. From an attempt to cut off the left wing of 64th Army, it had now become possible to grasp a much bigger prize – the *right* wing of 64th Army and perhaps the whole of 62nd Army as well. All that was required was for IV Panzer Army to abandon its proposed right wheel, and continue northwards, while VI Army should come down to meet it. If this move succeeded, Stalingrad would be bound to fall this time, for lack of troops with which to defend it; but Army Group B would have to act quickly, for Yeremenko had already smelt a rat.

General Weichs, commanding Army Group 'B' reacted fast to the new situation, and at noon on August 30th transmitted an order to VI Army in which he said 'everything now depends on VI Army concentrating strongest forces possible . . . launching an attack in a general southerly direction . . . to destroy the enemy forces west of Stalingrad in co-operation with IV Panzer Army . . . ' On the following day he again urged him to move 'It is important that a quick link-up be made between the two armies, followed by a penetration into the centre of the city.'

But Paulus would not move. However far short of his expectations Yeremenko's counterattacks had fallen, they had persuaded both Wietersheim and Paulus that their northern front was in a very precarious situation. The Soviet counterattacks had not yet petered out, and Paulus considered that if he detached his fast forces for a drive to the south, his northern front might well collapse. Not until September 2nd did the Soviet pressure on Paulus relax; then he at once sent his tanks off to make contact with Hoth. On September 3rd, Seydlitz's infantry also made contact with the forward elements of IV Panzer Army, and a neat encirclement operation had been carried out. There was only one thing wrong; the Red Army had escaped again. What had happened?

Yeremenko had not realised that Hoth was after the *left* wing of 64th Army, and had unwittingly read the German mind *before* it changed, so by the time Weichs and Hoth had changed their plans and decided to exploit their unexpected success by going north instead, the Headquarters of Stalingrad Front was already feverishly issuing a stream of orders, which amounted to an abandonment of the outer perimeter of the Stalingrad defences. The right wing of 64th Army began to pull back on the night of August 29th-30th, most of it going into the middle defence line, while two divisions (29th and 204th) were withdrawn into Army reserve, and 62nd Army began to disengage on the following night, taking up positions in the middle defence zone north of 64th. It was not exactly a victory; rather it was a 'Dunkirk', for the *cordon sanitaire* around the city had been given up, and the Germans now pressed hard on Stalingrad from all directions.

But by an odd combination of premature optimism and second-guessing, Yeremenko had managed to save his main forces. His counter-attacks had on the whole been a failure except in one vital respect; they had pinned Paulus down for the vital days from August 30th to September 2nd; his guess about the German intentions was wrong at the time he made it, but in effect he spotted their opportunity before they did, so 62nd and 64th Armies lived to fight another day. But how many more days? It had been touch and go this time, and the renewed German pressure in the southern sector forced an immediate withdrawal from the intermediate to the inner defence zone on September 2nd. Here for the first time the Germans used self-propelled guns; though Yeremenko says they did not achieve the desired result, he hastens to point out that he immediately asked Stalin for some. Clearly he was worried about the effect of these weapons on troops who had never seen them before, and whose room to manœuvre was daily becoming more and more restricted.

The city now presented a terrible picture of destruction. It had been under almost continuous air attack since August 23rd, and the bombardment on September 2nd was especially heavy. The fires burning in Stalingrad could be seen many miles away over the steppe; worse from the military point of view was that the ferries over the Volga, now the only means of sustaining the Soviet forces, were under constant bombardment, not only by aircraft but also by artillery. At night, the Germans illuminated the river with flares, causing further hardship to the Soviet command, which had already been forced to give up daytime ferrying almost entirely. But luckily the wind sometimes carried the flares away, sometimes they were too low, too high, too near or too far away to be useful to the artillery spotters of VI Army, and somehow or other the stream of ammunition, food, and reinforcements kept coming, as come they must; 62nd and 64th Armies had been in almost continuous action since mid-July, and inevitably were short of manpower and equipment by the beginning of September. Furthermore, the next stage of the battle – the fighting on the inner defence line was about to begin.

'Every German must feel he lives under the muzzle of a Russian gun'

It had now become inaccurate to describe the northern part of Yeremenko's area as 'Stalingrad Front', as it was cut off from the city, except for 62nd Army. This army was therefore placed under the jurisdiction of South-East Front, so that there was one Army Group north of the German breach – Stalingrad Front, stretching about 250 miles from Babka on the Don to Yerzovka on the Volga, with five armies (1st Guards, 21st, 24th, 63rd and 66th), and one south of it – South-East Front with four armies (62nd in the city, 64th and 57th to the south of it and further south still, 51st Army, defending the fairly quiet sector behind the lakes of Tsatsa, Barmantsak, and Sarpa, below which the front line petered out into the Kalmyk Steppe, penetrated only by an occasional patrol from each side. It was impossible and perhaps imprudent to try to administer such a large military establishment from the underground bunker in the Tsaritsa ravine, a few miles from the front line, and so Yeremenko and Khrushchev departed quietly across the Volga, moved some 25 miles north and then crossed back to the west side, where they established their headquarters in the village of Malaya Ivanovka. There the might of Stavka descended upon them at the beginning of September, in the form of the Deputy Supreme Commander (the redoubtable General Zhukov), and the Chief of General Staff, Colonel-General Vasilevsky. They asked questions, they probed, they visited the front line, they even examined the bridgeheads over the Don, though why they did so, they told no-one, not even Yeremenko. In fact, before they left Moscow Stalin had told them to examine the possibility of using the bridgeheads as the bases for a great counteroffensive, and to tell nobody what they were up to. In 1920 the White forces of General Denikin had been defeated here by such a movement, and it had been to a large extent Stalin's own plan, so old memories were stirring as he looked at the General Staff maps and Paulus' extended northern flank.

But when he looked at the situation map for September 2nd, the idea of a grand *coup de main* vanished for the moment from his mind. That would

take time to prepare, and from the look of things Stalingrad was not going to hold out long enough for it, so he dashed off a message to Zhukov at Ivanovka.

'The situation at Stalingrad is getting worse. The enemy is three versts [about two miles] from Stalingrad. Stalingrad may be taken today or tomorrow if the northern group of forces does not give immediate help. Require the commanders of the forces deployed north and north-west of Stalingrad to strike at the enemy at once, and go to help the Stalingraders. No procrastination is permitted. Procrastination now equals crime. Throw all aviation in to help Stalingrad. In Stalingrad itself there are very few aircraft left.

Report receipt and measures taken without delay.

J. Stalin.'

The word 'Stalingrad' recurs like a drum beat throughout the message. Often Stalin's senior commanders could argue with him, but not this time; he wanted something done at once with the two armies (24th and 66th) which had just arrived in the Samofalovka – Yerzovka – Loznoye area from Stavka reserve. True, they were not yet fully trained, and they consisted mostly of older reservists (the prodigal way in which Soviet manpower had been squandered in 1941 and in operations such as the Kharkov offensive of May 1942 was still having its effects), but they had not been in action much as yet, and therefore were much nearer their full strength than those south of them, so they were put into the attack on September 5th, in yet another effort to pinch out the German salient between Don and Volga.

They did not succeed, but the Germans had to divert some of their efforts northwards to beat them off, and this took some of the pressure off 62nd and 64th Armies as they endeavoured to organise some kind of defence line around the perimeter of Stalingrad. The 'inner defence line' *sounded* good enough, but in many places it was no more than a line on Yeremenko's map. Wire had to be put down, mines laid, trenches and foxholes dug, all sorts of things had yet to be done. Nor was there an excess of

manpower available, as many of the rifle divisions were barely equal to a company at full strength; 87th had 180 men left, 112th had 150; 99th Tank Brigade had 120 men and no tanks.

This situation finally got the better of the commander of 62nd Army, General Lopatin. He had been growing steadily more pessimistic as the battle wore on, though he had performed creditably up to now, but with the Volga at his back and superior enemy forces before him, his will began to crack. He decided Stalingrad could not be held, and began to withdraw his units without orders, so there was nothing for it but to dismiss him. For the time being his Chief-of-Staff, Major-General N I Krylov took over command, but good Chiefs-of-Staff are almost as hard to find as good army commanders, so this arrangement could only be temporary and Yeremenko cast about for a successor among the generals on the spot.

At 64th Army HQ, there was no command problem. Major-General M. S. Shumilov had commanded the army since July 30th, and was a competent, calm, and untemperamental man, not given to extremes of optimism or pessimism. As his Deputy he had Lieutenant-General Vasily Ivanovich Chuykov, who had himself been the commander of 64th Army when it was a reserve army assembling and training around Tula, and who had been its commander from the time it arrived in the Stalingrad area until Shumilov took over from him. He was by no means the 'fifth wheel on the car', but since command of the army was in Shumilov's capable hands, Chuykov could be spared, and so it was that Chuykov was chosen to command 62nd Army, thus becoming in the eyes of the Soviet public the outstanding figure of the Stalingrad defence.

Chuykov was then aged forty-two. He had been Military Attaché in China at the outbreak of war, and had been back only since March 1942. Until July he had seen no action, but he had since acquitted himself well. He was decisive, conscientious and an optimist. Of course, Stalin had to ratify the appointment, but his only question of Yeremenko was 'Do you know him well enough?' Yeremenko answered that Chuykov was known to him as a leader on whom one could rely, and Stalin confirmed the proposal to give him 62nd Army, so he took over on September 12th.

Chuykov, by his own testimony, had been studying German battlefield tactics closely during his few weeks in action. Though he admired the polished way in which they co-ordinated their aircraft, tanks, and infantry, he was by no means over-awed by them, considering them often sluggish and irresolute. On taking over an army soon to be completely isolated on right and left, with a broad river at its back, and a superior command sufficiently far away not to be able to supervise his every move, he would have far more freedom of action than a Soviet army commander normally possessed, and therefore his views on how his army should fight are of more than ordinary relevance.

He believed that German methods derived their extraordinary success mainly from the excellent coordination of elements – aircraft, tanks and infantry – not in themselves of outstanding quality. In the fighting on the Don and Aksay rivers he had noted that until the Luftwaffe was over the Soviet positions, the tanks would not attack, and until the tanks had reached their objectives the infantry would not go in, so the problem as he saw it, was essentially one of breaking the chain, by whatever means; and he had also noted a certain dislike of the German infantry for close combat, observing that they would often open up with automatic weapons from half a mile's distance.

Putting together these two factors— – dependence on co-ordination and dislike of close combat – he arrived at the conclusion that the correct way to fight was to keep as close to them as possible. That way the Luftwaffe would be unable to attack the Soviet forces without putting its own troops at hazard, so the chain would be broken at its first link, and the infantry forced to fight in the close combat which he believed them to dislike against an enemy who had not first been softened up by bombers and tanks. As he himself later put it 'Every German soldier must be made to feel that he was living under the muzzle of a Russian gun'. It seemed to him that inside the city these tactics would be easy to apply, and the Germans would be deprived of their trump card – the Luftwaffe, providing, of course, that his own troops were willing and able to come to grips with the Germans at close quarters.

Chuykov's introduction to his new army was neither auspicious nor designed to give him confidence that his ideas could be applied. To begin with, no-one had any idea where its headquarters were. Yeremenko believed it to be in the Tsaritsyn bunker, the underground command post in the Tsaritsa ravine until recently occupied by himself and his Front headquarters, but it was not there, so Chuykov wandered about the city, marvelled at the makeshift barricades in the streets – incapable of keeping out a lorry, much less a tank – and finally found an officer who knew where 62nd Army's command post was. He guided Chuykov to the foot of the Mamayev Kurgan, and the new commander scrambled up the hill to Krylov's dug-out, where he found the Chief-of-Staff on the telephone telling off the commander of an armoured formation who, without orders, had withdrawn to the bank of the Volga from Hill 107.5 (Soviet practice was to designate hills by their height in metres as marked on the army maps), thus putting his headquarters behind that of the Army.

Clearly, if this was allowed, it would be the end of Chuykov's plans to fight the Germans at close quarters, so the unfortunate General in charge of the armour was sent for, told by Chuykov personally that he was guilty of cowardice, that any future act of this kind would be treated as treason and desertion, and given until 0400 hours to put his command post back on hill 107.5. When the Deputy Front Commander, General Golikov, arrived, the armour commander was put through the wringer once again for good measure.

Chuykov's first request to Golikov was for several additional divisions. He was faced by a total estimated at between eleven and fourteen German divisions, with reinforcements, supported by approximately one thousand aircraft of Luftflotte IV, against which

62nd Army had a motley collection including three armoured brigades with one tank between them (the two with no tanks were soon moved across the Volga to re-equip and reform), several infantry divisions each about equal to a full-strength battalion, Colonel Sarayev's 10th NKVD Division (more or less up to strength but short of heavy weapons) and two infantry brigades also near full strength. Their supporting air forces were completely dominated by Luftflotte IV, which gave the Germans complete air superiority, and to make matters worse, the ex-commander of 62nd Army, General Lopatin, completely broken in spirit, was still hovering around Army headquarters, continuing to infect his former subordinates with his pessimism.

Chuykov persuaded him to bow himself out of the battle, but the damage was done, for soon the Deputies to the Army Commander for Artillery, Tanks, and Engineering, pleaded illness and disappeared across the Volga. Intensive work by the Communist Party organisations in the Army, by the Political Department, by the Generals themselves, and a rousing message from Yeremenko and Khrushchev, did something to restore flagging morale, but still more was needed. Golikov's representations had been effective, and a stream of reinforcements was on its way – no less than ten infantry divisions, two Armoured Corps and eight Armoured Brigades were scheduled to arrive from Stavka reserve in the fortnight beginning on September 13th, and at least half of the infantry was assigned to 62nd Army. Indeed, it was to receive 10,000 men and 1,000 tons of supplies in the next three days.

To ensure the safe arrival of these reinforcements, it was essential to protect the very vulnerable landing stages, which at present were well within range of the German guns, 62nd Army's bridgehead being only three miles wide at its narrowest point. Besides, an attack suited Chuykov's temperament, as it would bring his men into close contact with the Germans and make it difficult for the Luftwaffe to operate against them.

Lieut. General A I Chuykov in command

As far as he was concerned, no-man's-land should not be wider than a grenade-throw.

He and Krylov stayed up until 0200 hours planning the attack. The army would defend actively on its right and left flanks, and its centre would attack to recapture Razgulyayevka station and the railway line south-west of it as far as the sharp bend near Gumrak, where it would consolidate, using the railroad embankment as an anti-tank obstacle, and then advance to Gorodishche and Alexandrovka. The necessary regrouping would be carried out at once, and the attack launched on the following day, September 14th.

Conscious of a job well done, Chuykov went to bed. At 0630 hours he was awakened by the crash of bombs and shells. The Germans had forestalled him.

What had happened was that Seydlitz' 51st Army Corps had been launched into a two-pronged attack against central Stalingrad, south-east from Gorodishche and north-east from Peschanka with two Panzer, one motorised, and three infantry divisions. By afternoon the forward Soviet defences had been overrun and the Machine-Tractor Station, its housing estate, and that of the airfield captured, while the southern prong was barely being held off from Kuporosnoya and the bank of the Volga. Worse, Chuykov had only the vaguest idea what was going on, as his command post at the top of the Mamayev Kurgan had been under continuous bombardment all day by German guns and mortars, its communications almost completely knocked out, and by 1600 hours he had almost no contact with his troops.

Even Chuykov, a man given to studied understatement, describes the situation as 'somewhat disquieting'. As it happens, the Germans were being held off at the western edge of the 'Barricades' and 'Red October' factories' housing estates, but this he did not know. All he knew was that it was impossible to direct the battle from this command post, so after hastily drawing up a plan for a limited attack the next morning he and his staff departed foodless (breakfast had been blown up by a bomb, dinner had received a direct hit from a mortar)

Left: Covering barrage. *Left below:* The infantry go in. *Below:* The first penetration

Luftwaffe troops
flush out a shelter
Top right: Factories
were prime targets
Middle right: Burnt
out hangar. The
airfield was soon in
German hands
Bottom right:
Stalingraders
watch the gradual
incursion

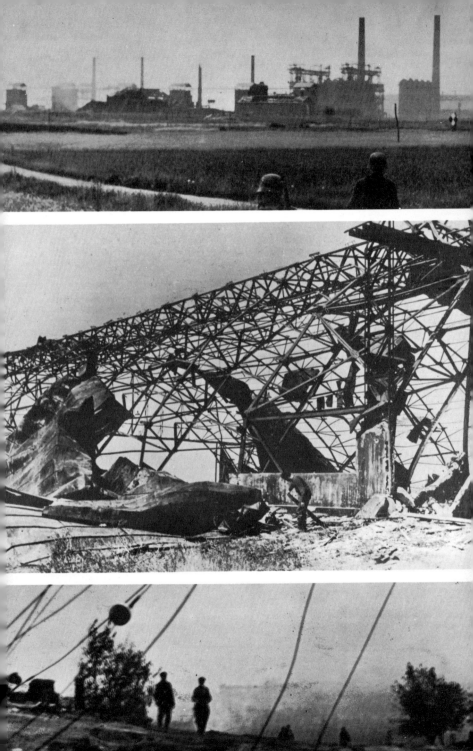

for the Tsaritsyn Bunker. Here they were able to remain for only three days, which was unfortunate, for it offered much better protection than the dug-outs on the Mamayev Kurgan, being 30 feet below ground level, and having much more space.

These were important considerations as this battle was not and could not be directed by remote control. The bridgehead was so small that reactions to enemy moves had to be quick and operations could not be controlled from the far bank of the Volga – apart from anything else, the Red Army had none of the special waterproof cable required for carrying its telephone communications across the Volga, and its signals troops had to use ordinary insulated cable, which required renewal every few days. Maintaining contact betwen 62nd Army headquarters, Front HQ at Ivanovka, and the elements of 62nd Army support arms (artillery, aircraft and supply services) on the east bank proved difficult enough, so the extra load to be carried if 62nd Army HQ had moved east of the Volga would probably have proved too much

There was, of course, radio; but that could be jammed, or worse, the messages passed over it monitored by the efficient German intercept services, and besides, radios were every bit as hard to come by as waterproof telephone cable –. most tanks were still without them. In any case, for a general of Chuykov's temperament, personal contact with his troops was important, so as Zhukov had done before him, during the defence of Moscow, he maintained his command post in the threatened area so that the morale of his troops would not be adversely affected by the sight of their general departing.

The HQ Staff arrived at the bunker shortly before 0300 hours on September 14th. At 0300 hours the Army's artillery began bombarding the German positions, and half an hour later the counterattack began. Chuykov at once telephoned Yeremenko to advise him of the fact and ask for air cover from dawn onwards. The Front Commander agreed, and gave Chuykov the welcome news that reinforcements were on the way; Major-General A I Rodimtsev's 13th Guards Rifle Division would be assembling during the day at the Volga ferry terminal near Krasnaya Sloboda. At once Chuykov despatched a group of staff officers to meet the division, then he and Krylov turned back to their immediate task – the counterattack.

The news was bad; the counterattack had failed, and the Germans were again advancing, making for the Central Station (Stalingrad-1). If they occupied it there was a serious danger that they would slice through 62nd Army and seize the central landing stage before Rodimtsev's division could arrive. Stalingrad's fate again hung in the balance as lorry-loads of German infantry poured into its centre behind the Panzer spearheads. Indeed, many of the Germans appear to have thought the city as good as taken, and Chuykov's men saw 'drunken Germans jumping down from their lorries, playing mouth-organs, shouting like mad and dancing on the pavements'. The front line was little more than half a mile from Army HQ, and the ferry terminal was endangered.

Chuykov's last reserve of 19 tanks was on the southern outskirts of the city. He ordered one battalion – nine tanks – to come to the command post, and while awaiting its arrival Krylov formed two assault groups from the staff officers and the headquarter guard. When the tanks arrived, two hours later six of them, with one of the assault groups were sent to block the streets leading from the railway station to the landing stage, and the other three, with the second group, to recapture a group of buildings known as the 'specialists' houses', where the Germans had installed heavy machine-guns covering the landing stage and the river.

At 1400 hours Rodimtsev arrived, after a perilous journey through the city from the landing stage, to report and receive instructions. His 13th Guards Division was near full strength, with about 10,000 men, but was short of weapons and ammunition. In particular over a thousand of his men had no rifles, and though Golikov had been instructed to deliver the necessary weapons to the Krasnaya Sloboda area by evening, there was no guarantee that they would arrive before the division began to cross to the city. Chuykov immediately gave orders for weapons belonging to 62nd Army's supply personnel on the east bank to be collected and delivered to Rodimt-sev's guardsmen, while Rodimtsev was instructed to bring his anti-tank guns and mortars over, but to leave his other artillery on the east bank, where it could do its job in greater safety, under direction from spotters in the city.

Rodimtsev was given the sector from Mamayev Kurgan in the south to the Tsaritsa river on the north, and the tasks of clearing the Germans from the city centre, the specialists' houses and the railway station with two of his regiments, while a third was to hold the Mamayev Kurgan and a battalion of infantry remain at Army HQ as a reserve. Chuykov told him to set up his command post in some existing dug-outs on the Volga bank, and when he objected to taking up his

Chuykov's command became firmer, the Russian defence took shape

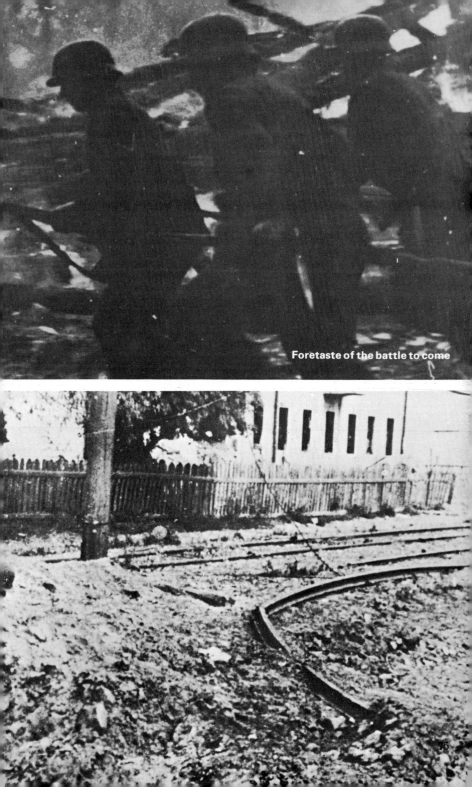

Foretaste of the battle to come

headquarters behind those of the Army, blandly assured him that once he had carried out his assignment he could move his command post forward.

Rodimtsev departed to make his arrangements. His division would begin to cross at dusk, in about five hours' time. It was now 1600 hours, and Chuykov's shattered divisions would have to hold on for another ten to twelve hours. There were no reserves left – even the staff officers and HQ guard were in action. The only possibility was Colonel Sarayev's NKVD division, but this did not consist of Army troops, and there was no love lost between Sarayev and the Army Commander. On the one hand, Chuykov was contemptuous of the 'fortifications' – blockhouses and barricades – which Sarayev as 'commander of Stalingrad garrison' had put up, while Sarayev for his part was disposed to treat Chuykov as an equal, not a superior, until finally Chuykov had to 'pull rank' on him. 'Do you understand, your division has been incorporated into 62nd Army. You have to accept the authority of the Army's Military Council without argument. Do you want me to telephone Front HQ to clarify the position?'

Sarayev conceded the point. 'I consider myself a soldier of 62nd Army', he replied.

So that point was cleared up, but there was still the main problem of reserves. It was clear that none of the NKVD troops could be spared; however, Sarayev had under his command a number of armed police, firemen, and factory workers. They were short of weapons, but there were about 1,500 of them, so Chuykov gave orders to Sarayev to select some solid buildings, especially in the city centre, fortify them, instal 50–100 men in each, and defend them to the bitter end. Weapons and supplies could be drawn from 62nd Army.

News from the front line was sporadic, and often the easiest way to gauge the progress of the fighting was to go to the Pushkin Street exit and listen. Keen ears were not needed – the German 71st Infantry Division was within 500 yards of the bunker. The line now seemed to be holding, though only just. One of Chuykov's regimental commanders had been missing since morning, and so delicately poised was morale that no one could be certain that he had not simply run out on his men.

Just before dusk, Major Khopko arrived to report that his last tank had been put out of action near the station. Chuykov packed him off back to his post with orders to hold on with the hundred or so men he had left, and the tank – which could fire, though it could not move – until relieved by men from Rodimtsev's division 'or else . . .'

The fighting began to subside as dusk fell, so Chuykov and his staff took stock of the position. The Germans had advanced as far as the Mamayev Kurgan and the railway line, and had reached the Central Railroad Station, though they had not yet captured it. They had occupied many buildings in the city centre, almost wiped out the units in 62nd Army's centre, and destroyed the Observation Post on Mamayev Kurgan. On the southern sector they had been held, but all the signs were that they were preparing to attack again.

All night long 62nd Army HQ buzzed with activity as officers came and went – some to fight, some to pin down the Germans in the specialists' houses and round the station so that they would be too busy to interfere with the disembarkation of Rodimtsev's troops; others still to and from the landing stage to meet the incoming battalions and lead them to the front line.

Despite all their efforts, it did not prove possible to bring the entire division across that night, but rather more than two-thirds of it was brought over and went immediately into position, though none too soon: the German attack was renewed the next morning, with elements of three divisions (71st, 76th, and 295th) attacking the station and the Mamayev Kurgan, while in the southern sector the expected German attack duly materialised, mounted by units of XIV and XXIV Panzer and 94th Infantry Divisions. The Luftwaffe was extremely active, and Rodimtsev's troops were heavily engaged before they had even got their bearings. The railroad station changed hands four times during the day, but was back in Soviet hands by nightfall, though elsewhere the battle went better for the Germans. They held the specialists' houses, despite furious and repeated attacks by the 34th Regiment of Rodimtsev's division supported by tanks, thus retaining the ability to machine-gun the central landing stage, and also inflicted heavy losses on Colonel Batrakov's infantry brigade and accompanying elements of the NKVD Division, forcing them back to the forestry station, while Dubyansky's Guards division was forced back to the western outskirts of the city south of the Tsaritsa river.

The battle for the Mamayev Kurgan went on all day with varying fortunes. This insignificant hill, marked as Height 102.0 on both German and Soviet maps dominated the entire city centre, so both sides were to set great store by it, and right up to the end of the Battle of Stalingrad possession of it would be contested, so fiercely that

it remained free of snow throughout the winter – the heat of exploding shells and bombs made it too hot for snow to lie. The Guardsmen of Rodimtsev's division were locked in a fight to the death with elements of three German divisions (XXII Panzer, 71st, and 295th Infantry) throughout September 15th, and by evening it began to look as if they would be forced off it, so Chuykov ordered the remaining regiment of the division (the 42nd) to be brought across the Volga that night and sent straight to the Mamayev Kurgan to be in position before dawn.

Apart from the problems of the front line, Chuykov was now directing the defence under severe physical difficulties, for German machine-gunners had moved into the valley of the Tsaritsa and had the Army HQ in their sights, so that it was dangerous to go outside. The HQ Guard was again in

It was not to fly over all of Stalingrad

action near the bunker and wounded were being brought into it. To add to the congestion inside, the morale of some of the weaker vessels began to crack towards evening and large numbers of officers and men made excuses to come in on 'urgent business' so that they could shelter from the incessant bombing and gunfire. The bunker had no ventilation system, and the atmosphere inside became intolerable, so Chuykov ordered a secondary command post to be set up on the bank of the Volga opposite the south end of Zaitevsky Island to assist in controlling the units of the army's right wing in the northern part of the city.

Again the fighting eased off during the night. The 42nd Regiment came over the river and took up positions at the foot of the Mamayev Kurgan alongside the men of the now very weakened 112th Rifle Division, and at dawn the artillery pounded the German positions for ten minutes, then the 42nd with one regiment of 112th Division advanced into a hurricane of mortar fire and bombs. A short though vicious hand-to-hand struggle settled the issue, and the Soviet troops began to dig in again on the summit, but the battle had been a costly one, and when the leading platoon reached the top of the hill, six men were left of the thirty who had begun the ascent, while the losses in the formations behind them were almost as heavy. Nevertheless they succeeded in beating off the German counterattack which followed almost at once, and holding on to the vital height. The emphasis now shifted to the Stalingrad-1 Railroad station.

Here a battalion of Rodimtsev's Guards had been installed since crossing the river on the night of September 14th, and on the morning of the 17th they came under very heavy attack from a force of German automatic riflemen supported by about 20 tanks, which drove them out of the station and surrounding buildings. They regrouped, counterattacked, and recovered the lost ground, only to be driven out again. In all the area changed hands four times during the day, but when night fell, it was again in Soviet hands littered with burnt-out tanks and the bodies of hundreds of dead of both sides. Mutual exhaustion, as much as the approach of dark-

ness, brought the fighting at the station to an end for the time being.

That night, with his headquarters under harassing fire from machine-gunners of the German 71st Infantry Division, Chuykov left the Tsaritsyn bunker to move to a new command post. To move through streets infested with German machine-gunners and tanks was too dangerous. The party therefore crossed the Volga to Krasnaya Sloboda, moved by road to Ferry 62, then transferred to an armoured launch to recross the river to the new

Above: Russian patrol races to a threatened spot
Below: Strongpoint in the rubble
Above right: Where armour could move, it always won in this first stage
Below right: Where armour was blocked, light anti-tank guns blasted the buildings

site. On the way from Krasnaya Sloboda Gurov, the Army's 'Member of Military Council' suggested a meal and a bath, but while the Army Commander lingered over a cup of tea, the night began to pass away, and with it the opportunity of getting back to the other bank, since the ferries now worked only by night. A mad dash to the landing stage ensued, and Chuykov managed to leap from the bank to the last ferry, which had already left the landing stage. On arrival at the new command post he took

stock of the situation and found that several of his senior officers had 'disappeared' while on the eastern bank. Thus fragile was morale still.

The new command post was under the overhang of the Volga bank underneath some oil tanks. A number of sunken barges lay in the shallow water nearby, half above the surface, and in these the staff officers installed themselves, while the Military Council and Chief-of-Staff were put into some open trenches. All, for the moment, were in the open air, pending the building of dug-outs, which the sappers began on

at once and nobody knew whether the oil tanks were empty or not. It was a great come-down from the custom-built Tsaritsyn bunker, but that was no longer 'safe', if that word could be applied to any place in the bridgehead, and at least the new post was 1¼ miles from the front line.

At daybreak the Luftwaffe appeared again and the fighting was renewed, but at 0800 hours Richthofen's planes vanished; Stalingrad Front, north of the city, had begun a probing attack. However, it soon petered out, and by 1400 hours the German aircraft were back in force. During their absence the troops on the army's right flank improved their positions, and those on Mamayev Kurgan also gained 100–150 yards. In the centre the situation deteriorated somewhat and the railroad station, which had changed hands fifteen times in five days, finally fell to the Germans on the evening of the 18th, nor were there any reserves left with which to retake it, for the magnificent 13th Guards Division of General Rodimtsev had been reduced to a skeleton.

It had not been sacrificed to no purpose; unquestionably it had saved Stalingrad on September 14th, and even now individuals or groups of two and three men were fighting on in the basements, behind the platforms, or from under railway carriages and would do so night and day for some time to come. In so doing they would gradually change the whole character of the battle, bringing to life Chuykov's dictum that 'every German must be made to feel he is living under the muzzle of a Russian gun'. But as a large infantry formation they no longer existed, after the pounding to which they had been subjected during their first few days in the line.

In the area south of the city, Kuporosnoye fell, bringing the Germans out on the Volga at yet another place, completing the isolation of 62nd Army, hampering the work of the ferries even more, and creating a threat to the supply and artillery services which packed the far bank of the river; the artillery had become particularly important, because the continued shrinking of the bridgehead made it more and more impractical to maintain field-gun and howitzer regiments in the city itself, and Yeremenko was forced to assemble the fragments of units withdrawn to the east bank to regroup and reform into a defensive force covering the sector between Sredne-Pogromnoye and Gromki, opposite the sections of the bank held by the Germans.

The 62nd Army's position now appeared desperate, and in an effort to ease the pressure on it, Yeremenko mounted a full scale attack on September 19th, aimed at breaking through the German defences in the

Chuykov and Yeremenko possessed a large measure of the prima donna temperament often found in a successful military commander, and that Yeremenko's accounts of incidents in his wartime career have more than once been challenged by other generals, but on this occasion, it is doubtful whether Chuykov's allegations can be fully substantiated. He himself admits that Paulus had not yet committed the main forces of VI Army to the attack on the city, and implies that Stalingrad Front's

Inevitably, the advance slowed as it reached the factories

Gumrak-Gorodische area, and linking up with 62nd Army, which was to join in by attacking with three infantry divisions and an armoured brigade from the vicinity of the Mamayev Kurgan towards Rynok and Orlovka in the north-west and west of Stalingrad. This attack was a failure, and Chuykov has commented on Yeremenko's execution of it with some acerbity, alleging that it was prepared with undue haste, that the forces were illtrained and unduly dispersed, that it was launched at the wrong time and against the main forces of VI Army, which had not yet been worn down by the fighting in the city, and was launched in daylight despite the German superiority in the air.

Though he blames most of these faults on General Gordov, the former Front commander (who has been the recipient of almost as much blame for Soviet errors as Hitler has been for German ones), the allegations are aimed also at Gordov's superior, Yeremenko. It is true that both

counterattack should not have been mounted until he had done so.

It is doubtful, on Chuykov's own testimony as to the strength of his army on September 19th, whether it could have stood up to an all-out attack by VI Army long enough for a counterattack by Stalingrad Front to save the day. Nevertheless, it is true that the counterattack failed, and was repelled by VI Army without any transfer of forces from 62nd Army's front, apart from aircraft. Yet this argues only that the attack was badly executed, not that it was wrong to attempt it; and the two divisions which arrived as reinforcements specifically for the counterattack (Gorishny's and Batyuk's) were to prove as valuable as Rodimtsev's had been in the days that followed. Stalingrad Front renewed its attack on the 20th and at 0200 hours on the 21st Yeremenko rang up Chuykov warning him that an armoured brigade had broken through the German positions and would soon link up with 62nd Army in the Orlovka area. The 62nd Army staff sat up all night waiting for the link-up to be reported but Yeremenko's optimism proved premature – by four months and five days.

Most of the southern city was now in German hands, but on the southern outskirts stood a vast building: the grain elevator, defended by about 30 guardsmen, and 18 men of the 'Naval Infantry' (not marines, but sailors whom the High Command had pressed into service because of the manpower shortage). The sailors won a tremendous reputation wherever they were used, and most of the ones in the elevator were a particularly tough

tank support attempted on September 21st to break through to the left bank of the Tsaritsa river, and but for heavy fire from the artillery on the east bank of the Volga would have done so, and on the 22nd Rodimtsev's men were driven away from the central landing stage. Almost the whole of 62nd Army's rear was now open to German fire, while only the stages in the north of the city could now be used – and that only at night. Batyuk's newly-arrived division was given the task of liquidating the German force

. . . and the defenders fought back from the debris

breed from the Arctic, who were ordered to the elevator on the evening of the 17th to reinforce the garrison of guardsmen.

The elevator was attacked by a German battalion and the fighting went on for five days. In the end elements of three German divisions (XXIX Motorised, XIV Panzer and 94th Infantry) were drawn into the battle, but not until the 22nd, when hardly any of the garrison were left alive, and they had neither water nor ammunition, was the elevator captured. This action showed in microcosm how the German commitment to the taking of Stalingrad could be made to escalate, given firm defence by relatively small bodies of men; but the capture of the elevator meant that the southern part of the city was now for all practical purposes in German hands, though as in the railway station area small bodies of men continued to fight on in the German rear.

In the centre of the city, the situation was critical, German troops with

in the central landing stage area and taking firm control of the valley of the Tsaritsa.

Chuykov sent for Batyuk and briefed him on the use of small combat groups, as he was not sure in his mind that Batyuk had adapted himself away from the peacetime drills under which the units were much larger, until finally Batyuk (who had in fact taken note of the peculiarities of street fighting in Stalingrad before his division crossed the Volga, and made his dispositions accordingly) cut short his commander's harangue with a few well-chosen words, 'I've come to fight, not parade. My regiments have Siberians in them . . .', after which Chuykov left him to get on with the job.

Within an hour, at 1000 hours on September 23rd, Batyuk's men were put in to the attack down the Volga bank towards the landing stage, while Rodimtsev attacked northwards with 2,000 reinforcements, but the Germans were too well dug in, and two days of of fierce fighting failed to dislodge them. Nevertheless, Paulus was unable to extend his penetrations fur-

ther, and from the evening of the 24th
the fighting began to die down again.
The 62nd Army had been split in two,
but it was still in business.

Left and below: **The first stalemate**

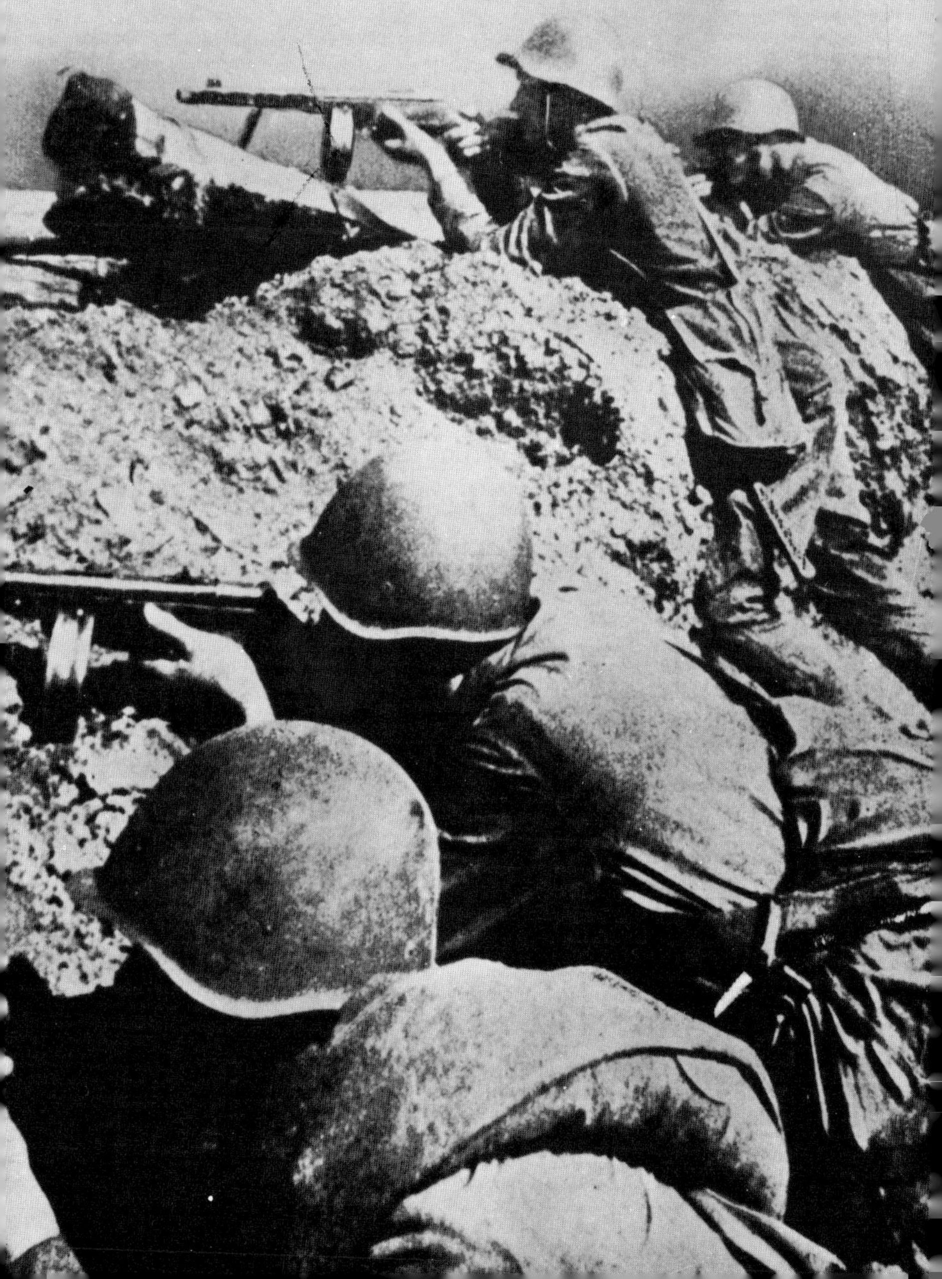

Hitler changes the team

While the battle had been raging over the ruins of Stalingrad, dramatic events had been taking place at Hitler's headquarters. The offensive against the Caucasian oilfields had also stalled short of its objectives, and the Führer, never very trustful of his generals, was looking for scapegoats; and so he had sent one of the few soldiers who enjoyed his confidence, Colonel-General Jodl of OKW, to the headquarters of Army Group A to find out why its C-in-C, Field Marshal List, was not making better head-way, Jodl returned to report that List had acted exactly in accordance with Hitler's own orders, but that the terrain and the strong Russian resistance had combined against him.

Hitler fell into one of his tempers and ordered Jodl's replacement, but in fact Jodl, who believed that 'a dictator, as a matter of psychological necessity, must never be reminded of his own errors, in order to maintain his self-confidence' never again violated his own dictum, and was not replaced. But List was, on September 10th. So was General von Wietersheim, commander of XIV Panzer Corps,

followed by General von Schwedler of IV Panzer Corps – the first for objecting to the use of Panzers to hold open the Rynok corridor from Don to Volga, a task more suitable for infantry, and the second for the 'defeatist' suggestion that the concentration of such strong forces at the tip of a salient with vulnerable flanks could be very dangerous for VI Army. These dismissals were, however, overshadowed by the departure of Colonel-General Halder, the Chief of General Staff at OKH on September 24th.

It was already time for the planners at OKH to turn their attention to the coming winter, and try to predict where the Red Army's winter offensive would be launched; and the majority opinion was that it would take place in the middle of the front; and so both Halder and the C-in-C Army Group Centre, Field-Marshal von Kluge, were anxious for reinforcements, which were not available because of the pressure of events in the south. New Soviet divisions were being identified on the central sector almost daily, would be active for a few days and then disappear, into reserve behind the centre as Kluge and Halder believed.

Personal relations between Hitler and Halder had been deteriorating for months, and a fairly trivial argument over these evanescent Soviet divisions grew out of all proportion, so that on September 24th Halder was dismissed. His successor, Zeitzler, was promoted over the heads of many senior and better generals; his *forte* was logistics. Hitler wanted a man who would move troops to where he, Hitler, said they should go, and Zeitzler would be good at that; so he joined the clique of pliable yes-men with which OKW and OKH were gradually being packed. Henceforward Hitler would exercise much more direct control than Halder had ever granted him.

Hitler's principal adjutant, General Schmundt, was promoted to head the Army Personnel Office, so Paulus (who throughout his career showed himself as good a courtier as a soldier) sent him congratulations; and this too was to have a disproportionate effect on the course of the Stalingrad battle, for Schmundt thereupon confided to him that he was being considered as a replacement for Jodl as Chief-of-Staff at OKW. Paulus was given to understand that a quick seizure of Stalingrad would advance his cause very considerably and so at once began to plan his return to the corridors of power through the ruins of Stalingrad – which was a pity, for his talents were essentially those of a staff officer rather than a field commander.

The argument about the vanishing Soviet divisions had more connection with Stalingrad than the Germans realised at the time. Though Stalin's court could be quite as Byzantine as Hitler's, Stavka on the whole lacked the atmosphere of feverish intrigue which enwrapped Hitler's headquarters. Sometimes glacially slow to move, it was on the whole a place of purposive contemplation rather than of frenzied activity, and Stalin interfered less with it than Hitler did with his General Staff. Like Schwedler, Stavka had become interested in the long exposed German flank along the Don, and as already mentioned, the Deputy Supreme Commander, Zhukov, and Chief of General Staff, Vassilevsky, had visited the Soviet bridgeheads across the Don early in September.

When they returned to Moscow they held a conference at which a preliminary plan for a counter-offensive was worked out, and it was in this connection that new Soviet divisions began appearing and disappearing on the central sector. They were being 'baptised' on the relatively quiet parts of the central front, then withdrawn, and the Germans were quite right to conclude that they were going into reserve. They were; but not in the centre. They were being dispatched to the Stalingrad area, for what was afoot was a giant pincer operation – the encirclement and destruction of VI Army, IV Panzer Army, and as many of the satellites as could be put in the bag.

The German attention must be kept concentrated on Stalingrad, and therefore the city must be held. But to treat Stalingrad as a mincing machine, as the Germans had done at Verdun in 1916, and as Paulus seemed prepared to do, was neither an elegant solution nor a possible one, given the Red Army's acute shortage of manpower. Besides, the bridgehead at Stalingrad was now so small that to pack large forces in there would raise appalling supply problems, and expose the closely-packed masses to a slaughter at the hands of the Luftwaffe and the German infantry – whose capacities, whatever the shortcomings of thier higher leadership, were very formidable.

The decision not to fight a battle of attrition was therefore not entirely voluntary, but in any case, such a battle would not appeal to Zhukov, the only Soviet senior commander to date who had shown how to turn a superior enemy to flight – at Moscow in the previous year – and who, to do so, had found it necessary to issue an order 'categorically forbidding' frontal attacks on strongpoints. So 62nd Army was reinforced enough to keep it as a going concern, but the overwhelming majority of the divisions sent to the south from Stavka reserve between September 1st and November 1st went not into the city but into concentration areas north of the Don bend. Chuykov's requirements were heavy, and he received the equivalent of ten divisions; but nearly three times that number – twenty-seven divisions – went into the assembly areas behind Stalingrad Front.

The command structure, too had to be reorganised. Yeremenko's dual responsibility was abolished, and the Fronts were confusingly renamed, Stalingrad Front becoming Don Front and being put under command of Lieutenant-General K. K. Rokossovsky, while South-East Front was rechristened Stalingrad Front, with Yeremenko retaining command of it, and a new Army Group, South-West Front, was established, under the command of Lieutenant-General N. F. Vatutin. At the appropriate time it would take up positions on the right of Rokossovsky's forces, but for the time being its existence was kept secret, and its troops remained behind the line, training, equipping – and preparing.

Success of the Soviet plan depended on two things; first, the general Stavka assessment that German strength was ebbing slowly, and that there would be no large strategic reserves available to throw in against the Soviet offensive when it was launched; and secondly, on the continued success of 62nd and 64th Armies in pinning down a large German force in the Stalingrad area. This in turn depended on 62nd Army's ability to hold the city, because once it fell VI Army would be in a position to divert forces, both its own infantry and the tanks of IV Panzer Army, to defend its northern flank.

The bridgehead on the Volga now comprised only the northern part of the city consisting of the Tractor Factory, the 'Barricades' ordnance plant, the 'Red October' steel works and a number of other smaller plants, stretching in a row along the bank of the Volga north of the Mamayev Kurgan, and with the housing estates for their workers directly west of them. Under the dual stimuli – hope of advancement and fear of the Russian winter, now beginning to announce its approach – Paulus launched his heaviest attack yet, on October 4th.

Though most of 62nd Army was in good heart, there were still from time to time serious problems of morale. In late September, Chuykov had begun to be suspicious of the reports coming by radio from two brigades which were cut off from the main body of the Army, and were fighting independently south of the Tsaritsa. On investigation he discovered that the commander, and headquarters staff of the formation had abandoned their men and installed themselves on Golodny Island in the Volga, where they were manufacturing false reports about the progress of the fighting, and transmitting them to Army HQ. Chuykov is silent about the punishments he inflicted, but they were probably extreme.

It was, however, too late for on September 26th one of the abandoned brigades left its positions, summoned the ferries, and fled across the river. The other was withdrawn before it could do the same, and ferried north to the factory district, where under new officers it subsequently performed well. However, the withdrawal had freed German hands on the left of 62nd Army, and preparations began for yet another major German onslaught on the Mamayev Kurgan, which was now the linch-pin of the southern end of Chuykov's precarious toe-hold in the city.

German confidence was now at its height, at any rate among the troops who did the actual fighting. Their air superiority was still almost absolute, for although two new Soviet air armies were deploying further north, they were being husbanded for the counteroffensive and not committed to battle for fear of giving the show away. New formations from Germany – mostly specialised units, such as engineers and flame-thrower detachments – were being brought in for the last heave, and no particular care was taken to camouflage the intention to mount new attacks. So cocky were some, particularly those who had not yet been in battle, that they would shout across to the Russian positions (which were frequently on the opposite side of a street, or in the next building 'Russ! Tomorrow bang-bang!', thus warning their embattled opponents and giving them time to take appropriate steps.

Those who went : *Top left :* Col. General Halder, Chief of the General Staff. *Top right :* Field Marshall List, C-in-C Army Group A. Those who came : *Bottom left :* Lieut. General KK Rokossovsky, Commander, Don Front. *Bottom right :* General NF Vatutin, Commander, South West Front

The bridgehead was now so small that almost all of it could be brought under fire from small arms, and movement in the open by day had become almost synomous with suicide. Gains or losses in battle were measured by the yard, and the basic unit of combat was the individual sniper or the storm group of mixed arms, usually automatic weapons, hand grenades, Molotov cocktails, machine guns and anti-tank rifles, or sometimes an anti-tank gun. This was not street fighting in the usual sense of the word, as to emerge in the open was usually too dangerous, and most of the fighting took place inside the ruined buildings. The storm groups were usually composed of assault groups of six to eight men each. Their job was to break into a building, and they were lightly armed with machine carbines, grenades, daggers, and spades (which were often used as axes as well).

They were supported by a reinforcement group, which would follow up as soon as the assault groups were inside, and establish a field of fire around the target to prevent the approach of enemy reinforcements. For this purpose the reinforcement groups were more heavily armed, with heavy machine-guns and automatic weapons, mortars, anti-tank rifles or guns, crow-bars, picks, and explosives. In addition, the reserve group was used to supplement the assault groups, to block off the flanks against enemy attack, and if necessary to cover the withdrawal of the assault and reinforcement groups. These highly specialised small units proved very successful, and the small size of the basic unit, the assault group, made it possible to construct storm groups of varying sizes and compositions according to the nature of the target.

In defence, the storm groups would be deployed with anti-tank weapons on the ground floor, machine guns on the higher storeys, and infantry at all levels including the basement. The 62nd Army, thanks to its specialised structure and tactics proved itself superior in close fighting, even against odds, and Paulus' neglect of the need to adopt special methods to meet the particular conditions showed yet again

The Street fighting
1. Russian assault group moves in
2. Once inside, the fighting was fierce and ruthless
3. Support group holds off enemy reinforcements
4. The Germans never became as skilful as the Russians. Luftwaffe troops arrogantly stand, inviting slaughter

the lack of resourcefulness with which the German leadership approached the situation. Against the skill and cunning of Chuykov's specialised tactics, his only answer was to concentrate more and more force at the tip of the salient – just where Zhukov wanted it.

Chuykov had succeeded in forging 62nd Army into a highly competent body of house-to-house fighters, and his tactic of keeping close to the enemy was paying off. On many of the sectors where the fighting was fiercest, the Luftwaffe was either reduced to impotance or reduced to bombing both sides impartially, but now all the indications were that a major German attack was impending. The 62nd Army would need all its skill and combativeness.

The indications from reconnaissance, and from the German carelessness over concealing their intentions, made it possible to deduce by September 26th that Paulus' offensive was to be mounted from the Gorodishche – Razgulyayevka direction against the housing estates of the 'Barricades' and 'Red October' factories, thence into the factories themselves and the Volga bank behind them. In the realisation that each successive German attack reduced still further his limited room to manoeuvre, and knowing that more reinforcements were on their way (General Smekhotvorov's 193rd Infantry Division would begin to cross the river on the evening of the 27th, followed on the 30th by the 308th Infantry of General Gurtiev and on October 3rd by General Zholudev's 37th Guards), Chuykov decided to try to disrupt Paulus' preparations by maintaining constant bombardment by the artillery group on the east bank, and strengthening the defences on the north side of the city, at present very weakly held by the thoroughly exhausted 112th Infantry Division and a much understrength tank brigade.

The situation at the Mamayev Kurgan was again causing anxiety, as the Germans were on its western and southern slopes, little more than one hundred yards from the top. A strong counterattack here would perhaps restore the position; it might even

disrupt Paulus' plan to attack the factory area by making him divert troops back to the centre of the city – and they would be vulnerable to artillery bombardment while in transit along the Gumrak-Stalingrad road. However, the bulk of the army would have to remain in position to withstand the Paulus offensive, and in the end only the understrength divisions of Gorishny, Batyuk, and Rodimtsev could be used.

Chuykov was still so apprehensive that his subordinates would revert to the peacetime practices of attack by large formations that in the order for the attack (Army Order No. 166 of September 26th) he found it necessary to state 'I again caution all unit and formation commanders not to execute combat operations with entire units such as companies and battalions. The offensive should be organised mainly on a small-group basis, with automatic weapons, hand grenades, bottles of inflammable mixture and anti-tank rifles . . .'

After a 60-minute artillery bombardment, the infantry moved out at 0600 hours on the 27th, but after some initial gains they were forced to go to ground by German dive-bombers about 0800. At 1030 a massive German assault began against the Mamayev Kurgan and the 'Red October' housing estate. Three German divisions, XXIV Panzer, 100th Infantry, and 389th Infantry, were involved, 100th a fresh division and 389th newly made up to strength. Chuykov had beaten Paulus to the punch by only four and a half hours, and the most critical period for 62nd Army had begun.

The Luftwaffe plastered the entire bridgehead with bombs and the strong point of Gorishny's 95th Division at the top of the Mamayev Kurgan was obliterated. Army HQ under the overhang of the Volga bank was under air attack throughout the day, and the open oil reservoir adjacent to the oil tanks above the HQ began to burn, covering the area with a pall of choking black smoke. Towards mid-day the telephones began to give trouble and the radio links to cease functioning. Clearly, there was serious trouble at the front line, but it was impossible to find out at HQ how bad it was.

The Leaders of 62nd Army therefore

dispersed to find out, Chuykov to Batyuk's division, Krylov to Gorishny's, and Gurov to the armoured formation. When they got back they found that many of their staff officers had decamped, so they compared notes as best they could, but it was well after nightfall by the time they had a full picture of the situation. In the north, the Germans had breached the minefields, overrun the forward positions of 112th Division and in places forced it back over a mile, penetrating the 'Barricades' housing estate, while in the centre, Gorishny's division had been driven off the Mamayev Kurgan with heavy losses, and what was left of it was hanging on precariously to the north-east slopes. 'One more battle like that' thought Chuykov, 'and we'll be in the Volga'.

Khrushchev rang from Front HQ, and Chuykov told him that in spite of all 62nd Army's efforts, German superiority in men and materials was beginning to give them the upper hand, but that his Military Council was working on ways to destroy the force battering its way into the city from the Razgulyayevka area.

'What help do you need?' Khrushchev asked.

'I'm not complaining about the air force, which is putting up a heroic fight, but the enemy has mastery of the air. The Luftwaffe is his trump card in attack. Therefore I ask for more help in this field – air cover, if only for a few hours a day'.

Krushchev replied that the Front was already doing all it could, but undertook to see if yet more could be done.

That night (September 27th–28th), unit commanders and political workers were sent out to the dug-outs and trenches to bring their men up to the highest pitch of resolve, while two of Smekhotvorov's regiments were ferried across and sent straight into the line on the western edge of the 'Red October' housing estate. The artillery shelled the Mamayev Kurgan all night, so that the Germans on the top would have no chance to dig in, and a counterattack by Batyuk's division and the remnants of Gorishny's was organised for the coming day.

The Luftwaffe came in again at dawn on the 28th, dropping everything

Above and below: The open oil reservoir hit by Luftwaffe 27th September

The black pall hung above the city all day

they could lay their hands on (there is no record of a kitchen sink being dropped, but pieces of metal, ploughs, tractor wheels, and empty cans fell by the hundred on the heads of Chuykov's men, along with the bombs). They maintained constant attacks on the troops, the ferries, and the Army HQ. Five of the six cargo ferries were put out of action, the flames from the burning oil tanks spread to the Military Council's dug-out, and Chuykov's personal cook, Glinka, was injured in the shell hole which he used for a kitchen.

Nevertheless, Chuykov detected grounds for hope. The German attacks seemed to him to lack co-ordination, and to be slower than in the past. Better still, Krushchev's promise to improve the air support had borne fruit, and the Air Commander, the 32-year-old Major-General Khryukin, gave 62nd Army the strongest air support it had yet received, under which the counterattack on the Mamayev Kurgan went in with some prospect of success. The summit was not recaptured, but was made untenable to the

Germans, and became for the time being a no-man's-land, under heavy artillery fire from both sides.

The fighting of September 28th therefore had gone reasonably well for 62nd Army, but its position was still precarious in the extreme, so Stavka reconsidered its earlier resolve to reinforce the 62nd Army area as sparingly as possible, especially since an attack on Kuporosnoye by 64th Army, made on September 27th, also failed, leaving 62nd Army isolated as before. Now reinforcements began to pour down to Stalingrad; but not infantry or tank divisions for 62nd or 64th Army. This time most of them were machine-gun battalions and 'fortified area' troops (static formations, mostly formed from older men, and intended primarily for static defence), and they were not intended for the city.

The order from Stavka was to fortify the islands in the Volga and the east bank between Sredne-Pogromnoye and Gromki. The artillery on the east bank was reorganised to form part of the defences, while continuing to

Below and right : By the end of September the Germans commanded the river crossings. *Far right :* Reinforcements are put into the line

support the troops in the city, and nine machine-gun battalions and one rifle division were despatched from Stavka reserve to the east bank. So was the 159th Fortified Area, with twelve battalions of machine-guns and artillery, and a number of other formations, including 43rd Engineer Brigade, which at once set about laying mines along the east bank.

If the Germans should break through here and charge north up the east bank, the Soviet divisions assembling west of the river behind the Don would be endangered. The grand plan for an encirclement operation would collapse, and the biter would be bit. So a fence must be put up *behind* 62nd Army.

Stavka was hedging its bets.

Now that most of the cargo ferries had been lost, the ferrying of men and ammunition across to the city was to become more difficult, and there were also large numbers of wounded, whom it had not been possible to evacuate during the night. And now fresh German infantry and tanks were being brought up to the 'Red October' settlement, and, the hitherto quiet 'Orlovka salient', on the Army's far right, was about to erupt.

The Orlovka salient jutted out north of the city for about five miles, and was about a mile wide at its neck, just east of Orlovka itself. The Germans around it (elements of XVI Panzer, 60th Motorised, 100th, and 389th Infantry Divisions) were primarily occupied with guarding the northern flank of VI Army against any attempt by Yeremenko to break through and relieve Stalingrad and as long as the Soviet troops *inside* the salient remained quiescent, the Germans were not too concerned about them. Chuykov for his part had no troops to spare for dramatic action in a relatively remote part of the sector held by 62nd Army, so he refrained from provoking the Germans in this area, and garrisoned it with relatively weak forces. Nevertheless, Paulus did see some danger in the continued existence of the salient. If Yeremenko should succeed in breaking through to it, his left flank on the Volga at Latashanka would be cut off, and if Chuykov should put any of his new

divisions into the salient, the flank of the German forces attacking into the factory area would be vulnerable.

With the initiation of the offensive in the northern part of the city, which would involve a major attack into the factory area, it was clearly time for Paulus to liquidate the Orlovka salient, and this he proceeded to do. The weak forces there were soon over-run, and in view of intelligence reports of concentrations of tanks and infantry from the German XIV Panzer and 94th Infantry Divisions in the Vishnevaya, 'Long' and 'Steep' gullies and 'Red October' cemetery, obviously in preparation for a renewed attack on the Tractor and 'Barricades' factories, Chuykov decided he could do nothing about the situation in the Orlovka salient, so he withdrew most of Andryusenko's infantry brigade, strengthened them with an anti-tank regiment and two companies from Gorokhov's brigade, and prepared to launch a counterattack in three days' time on the 'Barricades' housing estate.

Guryev's 39th Guards Infantry Division began crossing the Volga that night, September 30th. It was only at half strength, but proved to be of outstanding quality, so Chuykov decided to place it between the Silicate Factory and Zuyevskaya Street, as he planned to use it in the counterattack against the Barricades housing estate. However on the following day its neighbours on the left, Smekhot-vorov's division, suffered a severe reverse when the Germans drove a deep wedge into their positions and appeared likely to break through into the 'Red October' factory, and the decision was then taken to deploy the 39th Guards behind Smekhotvorov's men, with orders to turn the factory buildings into strongpoints. On October 1st the German pincers met on the Orlovka salient, cutting off Andryusenko's 3rd battalion, the only one which had not been withdrawn. The battalion had only 200 rounds per rifle and two days' food. In spite of that it held on for five days, and on October 7th 120 survivors managed to get back to 62nd Army's lines, leaving 380 dead and wounded behind them.

The position of 62nd Army was now deteriorating rapidly. Smekhot-vorov's division had been in serious

Now the factories became the centres of battle

trouble ever since its arrival; it had lost three regimental and three battalion commanders on its first day, and after less than a week in action was down to less than 2,000 men. Fortunately another division of reinforcements was already assembling across the Volga, Colonel Gurtyev's 308th Infantry, mostly Siberians. On Batyuk's and Rodimtsev's sectors in the city centre, the Germans were just about being held, but were intensifying their pressure. A battalion of Germans disguised in Red Army uniforms had attempted to penetrate down the 'Steep' Gulley to the Volga, but had been detected and wiped out, Smekhotvorov's division was being pushed back, the Germans were getting closer to the 'Red October' factory, and to add to Chuykov's problems his Command Post again came under attack.

More than a week previously the oil reservoir above it had caught fire, and ever since the post had been under a pall of oily black smoke, which made

the working conditions there almost intolerable, but at least provided a smoke screen to keep the Luftwaffe away. On October 2nd, however, a determined air and artillery attack was launched against the post, and this time the oil tanks themselves were burst open, engulfing the command post, the sunken barges and the Volga itself in blazing oil. The telephone lines went up in flames, the radio worked only intermittently, and there was no escape route, so Krylov ordered the staff into the intact dug-outs and told them to maintain contact with the troops by radio. The fire lasted for several days, the post remained under bombardment, and it was impossible to sleep, but perhaps the most irritating feature of those days, according to Chuykov, was to be called constantly to the radio by Yeremenko's Chief-of-Staff, General G F Zakharov, to answer pettifogging questions designed solely to establish whether the Army HQ still existed.

From now on the German pressure steadily intensified. Everywhere in the north of the city the Soviet perimeter was contracting slowly, and the 'Red October' factory came under direct attack, but so far Guryev's men were holding on; so were the divisions in the city centre. But now a new threat developed, when on October 4th Chuykov's patrols established the presence of three German infantry and two Panzer divisions on a three mile front between the Mechetka and Hill 107.5 north of it. The Tractor Factory was about to be attacked.

On the previous day Chuykov had been notified that 37th Guards Infantry Division (Major-General Zholudev) was to begin crossing to Stalingrad that night. It had to come across without its anti-tank guns, because of the shortage of boats, and, for some unexplained reason, its HQ could not cross that first night, so the regiments were placed directly under command of Army HQ and rushed into position to the right of Gurtyev's men, to defend the Tractor Factory. The next night they were joined by the light tanks of 84th Armoured Brigade – the medium tanks could not be ferried over. The light tanks were useless against the German Mk III and IV tanks, so they were dug in and used as static firing points.

The reinforcements had arrived only just in time, for scarcely had they reached their positions when the major German attack on the Tractor Factory was launched on October 4th, with elements of XIV Panzer, 60th Motorised and 389th Infantry Divisions. The 37th Guards stopped them in their tracks, and they made no progress at all. October 6th was quiet, as the Germans paused to regroup, and Yeremenko, taking this as a sign of German exhaustion, prodded Chuykov to use 37th Guards for a counterattack on the following day, but the counterattack never took place, because the Germans forestalled it with a full-scale attack by the two infantry divisions and a mass of tanks. The 37th Guards were pressed slowly back, exacting a heavy price for every foot of ground, and the main German gain of the day was – one block of flats in the Tractor Factory housing estate. At 1800 hours the *Katyusha* rockets scored a fortuitous but fantastic success, wiping out almost an entire German battalion west of the railway bridge over the Mechetka with one salvo. This brought Paulus' losses for the day to almost four battalions – a high price for a block of flats. He paused to reconsider.

The lull lasted for four days, but it was clear that fighting would be extremely hard when it resumed. Both sides regrouped, and 62nd Army prepared to meet the renewed attack on the Tractor Factory. Yeremenko ordered a counterattack against the western outskirts of the Tractor Factory settlement, which was launched by 37th Guards and one regiment of Gorishny's division on the 12th, and it is indicative of the tension between the main Soviet protagonists that Chuykov writes 'We did not expect any great results from the counterattack but felt that *on this occasion* the Front Commander was not asking 62nd Army to carry out active operations to no purpose' (author's italics). And his reason for giving Yeremenko credit for some sense 'on this occasion'? Simply that he had received notification that 62nd Army was soon

to be put on short rations of ammunition, always a sign to a Soviet commander' that a big offensive was to be mounted somewhere else. The most absolute secrecy was being maintained about the planned counteroffensive – Yeremenko himself had been informed of 'Plan Uranus', as it had been named, less than a fortnight previously – but this signal was unmistakable.

By the standards of Stalingrad the counterattack was quite successful, for Zholudev's men gained over 300 yards and Gorishny's about 200 – but that was as far as they could go. They fought for the whole of the 13th without gaining another inch and on the 14th, Paulus launched five divisinos, two of them Panzers, against the Tractor and 'Barricades' Factories.

October 14th was the supreme crisis for 62nd Army. The Luftwaffe flew nearly 3,000 sorties, while on the ground XIV and XXIV Panzer, 60th Motorised, 100th Infantry, and 389th Infantry Divisions stormed in against Zholudev's, Gorishny's, and Gurtyev's divisions and the 84th Armoured Brigade. Just before noon, part of Zholudev's line was overrun, and a group of about 180 tanks broke through, some making for the Tractor Facotry, others along the Mechetka to take the adjoining 112th Division in rear. Confused fighting went on all day, and by midnight the Germans had surrounded the Tractor Factory on three sides, and were fighting in the workshops. Around the walls lay some 3,000 German dead, East Prussians of XXIV Panzer Division and Hessian infantrymen of 389th Division, as well as untold hundreds of Zholudev's guards. That night the Volga ferries evacuated 3,500 Soviet wounded, the largest total for any single day of the battle.

The attack was renewed the next day, with the addition to the German force of 305th Infantry Division, as Paulus attempted to extend his gains north and south along the bank of the Volga. He was very near to success; 62nd Army had been split, the East Prussians of XXIV Panzer Division reached the bank of the Volga at the north end of the Tractor Factory, and

The Tractor Factory

Across the railways and through the factory yards the fighting grew ever fiercer

Chuykov's 'northern group' (three infantry brigades and the very few survivors of 112th Division) were encircled in Spartanovka; communications with them were only sporadic. Zholudev's 37th Guards Division had been forced away from the Tractor Factory, and what remained of it was fighting as separate garrisons, mostly in the Tractor Factory housing estate.

Gorishny's division was also in a bad way, and German infantrymen had slipped through to about 350 yards from the Army HQ. The telephone wires were in flames, not only at the Command Post but across the river at the emergency command post, thus threatening a complete breakdown of communication with the Army and Front Artillery on the east bank, so Chuykov was forced to consider the possibility that this time the Army HQ would be destroyed, and got through to Yeremenko, asking permission to transfer several sections of Army headquarters across the Volga, undertaking that he himself, Gurov and Krylov would remain in the city. Yeremenko refused. The sight of HQ packing up would be too much for the front-line troops at so crucial a moment.

So they stayed where they were, and by the night of October 16th, the Germans had been halted once again. Zholudev's and Gorishny's divisions lost 75 per cent of their men on October 15th, but so heavy were the losses of the German attackers, that Paulus' offensive again ground to a stop. He was running short of manpower – already he had had to call on other parts of Army Group B for reinforcements which could ill be spared, and even on the Replacement Army in Germany, and now he could expect no more reinforcements, while the Soviet barrel was not quite empty. One regiment of General Lyudnikov's 138th Rifle Division had already crossed into the city. The other two arrived on the night of October 16th-17th, and were at once sent to stiffen the sectors held by Zholudev's and Gorishny's divisions.

Chuykov did not feel he could disregard any sector of his front for long. He observed a large force of Germans collecting in a position from which

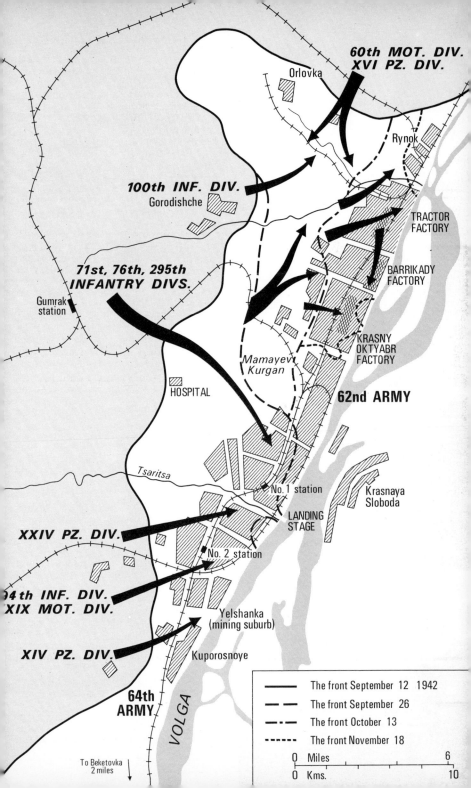

60th MOT. DIV.
XVI PZ. DIV.

Orlovka

Rynok

100th INF. DIV.
Gorodishche

TRACTOR
FACTORY

71st, 76th, 295th
INFANTRY DIVS.

BARRIKADY
FACTORY

Gumrak
station

KRASNY
OKTYABR
FACTORY

Mamayev
Kurgan

62nd ARMY

HOSPITAL

Tsaritsa

No. 1 station

Krasnaya
Sloboda

LANDING
STAGE

XXIV PZ. DIV.

No. 2 station

94th INF. DIV.
XIX MOT. DIV.

Yelshanka
(mining suburb)

XIV PZ. DIV.

Kuporosnoye

64th
ARMY

VOLGA

	The front September 12 1942
	The front September 26
	The front October 13
	The front November 18

To Beketovka
2 miles

0   Miles   6

0   Kms.   10

Below: The Attacker. *Right:* The Defender

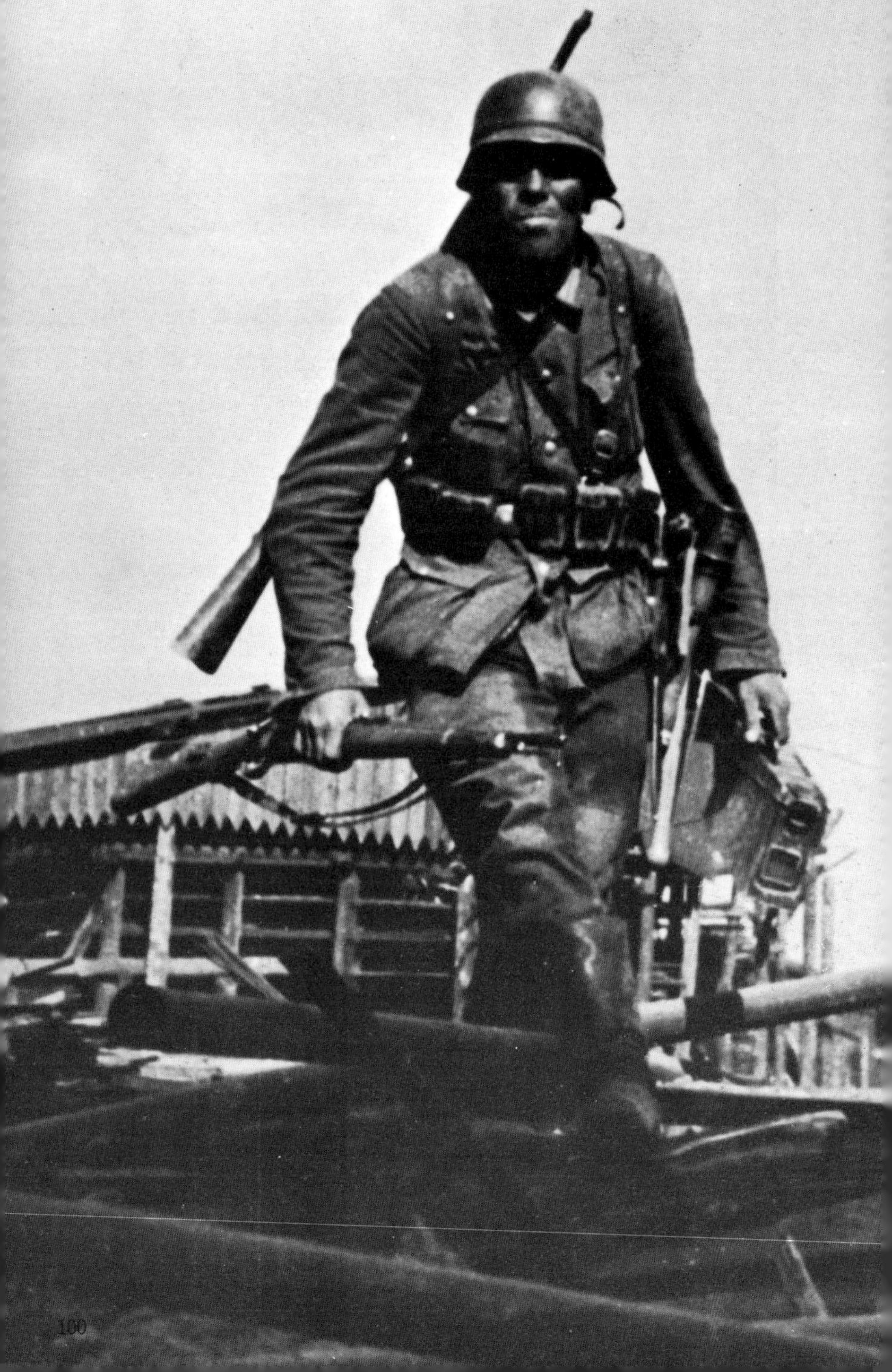

they could attack the 'Red October' factory, and had to make dispositions to meet this possibility, while on the quieter sectors to the south of the factory area, he was suspicious that Paulus was planning to make a surprise break while the bulk of 62nd Army was pinned down in the factory area, though actually he seems to have credited Paulus with too much subtlety here.

Yeremenko had spoken to Chuykov on the 15th, and being convinced (he does not say why, but the request to move part of the Army HQ across the river probably had something to do with it) that Chuykov's spirits had fallen (it would be a miracle if they had not, but Yeremenko's capacity for optimism in and out of season was notorious) decided to pay him a visit, and after one abortive attempt to get across, he succeeded at the second attempt. Chuykov was not very pleased to see him (throughout the battle he did his utmost to discourage visits from VIPs, which he considered a burden and a distraction, but the visit passed off without any overt unpleasantness, and Yeremenko left at dawn, granting Chuykov's request for more reinforcements (in small units, and not divisions) and ammunition. However, Chuykov's temper was not improved when the next day he was notified of an ammunition allotion for the next month which would last one day of heavy fighting; vigorous protests produced only a small increase. Clearly something very big incdeed was being planned.

On the night of the 17th, 62nd Army moved its command post yet again, to a spot on the river bank about half a mile south of the Banny Gully and the same distance from the Mamayev Kurgan. They would remain here until the battle was over. The Germans continued to make ground towards the 'Red October' factory on the 18th, and late in the morning overran Smekhotvorov's right flank, threatening to encircle some units of the adjacent Gurtyev division, so to prevent this, Chuykov ordered Gurtyev's men to withdraw some 200-300 yards, the first time that he had ordered a retreat in the city area since taking command of the army.

October 19th and 20th were relatively quiet by the standards of Stalingrad. The Germans continued to attack the isolated northern group at Spartanovka, and kept up the pressure on the factories, but without any significant success. Paulus was getting no more reinforcements, but could still redeploy troops from quieter sections of VI Army's long front, whereas reinforcements of 62nd Army presented much greater physical difficulties. Intelligence reported a new concentration of Germans in the 'Barricades' housing area, and 62nd Army's supply units had to be raided for fresh manpower. The farriers, tailors, cobblers, mechanics, and storemen were formed into infantry companies and ferried across to the city.

On October 21st the Germans came on against the 'Barricades' and 'Red October' factories, and 62nd Army's last ferries, but again with no success to speak of. The following day, however, the pressure intensified as Paulus threw in the 79th Infantry Division with tank support. By evening the Soviet line at the Barricades factory had been broken, the Germans were advancing on the factory along the railway sidings, and a company of automatic riflemen from 79th Infantry Division had reached the north-west corner of the 'Red October' steel plant. The following morning the pressure was again stepped up, and by late afternoon two-thirds of the 'Barricades' factory was in German hands while small groups of Germans with tommy-guns penetrated into the workshops of the 'Red October' plant.

The strength of both sides was ebbing away, as Paulus' divisions were

being eaten up in the fighting at the rate of one every five days, or even less in the factory area, and clearly he could not sustain his pressure indefinitely, while as against that, the Soviet forces in the city had been split, the Tractor Factory and most of the 'Barricades' had fallen to the Germans, and fighting was taking place inside the 'Red October' plant, where Soviet machine gunners inside the dead furnaces were trying to hold back the Germans at the other end of the foundry shop, while 37th Guards, 308th, and 193rd Infantry Divisions of 62nd Army had almost ceased to exist – between them they mustered only a few hundred men.

On the 25th the attack on the northern group at Spartanovka was renewed, the centre of the settlement was lost, and Gorokhov's troops fell back towards the river; but after two more days of fighting – in which guns of the Volga Flotilla of the Soviet Navy did great execution among the attacking Germans – VI Army was pushed back. Further south, matters boded ill for Chuykov, as troops of the German 79th Division pushed through towards the 'Red October' plant, and reached the HQ of Guryev's 39th Guards, into which they began lobbing hand grenades. Chuykov hurriedly dispatched a company of the Army HQ Guard which retrieved the situation, but could not get back to the command post, and they had to be left with Guryev's division at the 'Red October' works. Worse still, on the same day (October 27th), German machine-gunners reached a point between the 'Barricades' and 'Red October' plants less than 400 yards from the Volga,

bringing 62nd Army's last remaining ferry landing under direct German machine-gun fire.

Fortunately yet another division of Soviet reinforcements – Sokolov's 45th Infantry – had begun to cross during the previous night, and two battalions of it had managed to reach the city before dawn on the 27th. They were put into position between the two factories, with orders to keep the Germans away from the river, and this they succeeded in doing until evening, when on the left flank they were forced back about 110 yards. One day of fighting had cost 45th Division half the men of its first two battalions, and landing the remaining units of the divison would be very slow and difficult; it would take two to three days. But could 62nd Army hold out that long? Paulus now held nine-tenths of the city, and every inch of the Soviet-held tenth was under fire. Chuykov's men held only the Mamayev Kurgan, a few factory buildings, and a narrow strip of the Volga bank, several miles long but only a few hundred yards wide.

Incredibly, they did hold out, and even managed to mount a small counterattack with three patched-up tanks. Fighting continued until October 30th but the German attacks were growing weaker and weaker. The 62nd Army had outlasted Paulus again.

Detritus of battle

'There'll be a holiday in our street, too'

There were to be more attacks by VI Army, and more anxious moments for Chuykov, but none to match those which his army had already survived. It was clear that the German offensive would not reach the objectives set back in the spring, the winter would soon be setting in, and the attrition of the summer had left the Wehrmacht ill-prepared to face it. The men of 62nd Army did not know it, but already on October 14th Hitler had suspended offensive operations everywhere except at Stalingrad and on a small sector of the front in the Caucasus. They did know – not through official channels, for the most stringent security covered the preparations for the counteroffensive, but through the grapevine which operated as strongly in the Red Army as in any other – that something very big was in the wind. There was the reduction in their allotment of ammunition, the comings and goings of top brass from Stavka, Stalin's speech on November 7th, the 25th anniversary of the Revolution, with its cryptic statement 'There's going to be a holiday in our street, too'.

Yeremenko told Chuykov that the Germans were planning to discontinue their offensive against 62nd Army, and withdrawing troops from the city to the flanks and rear. They were not – yet – but a nod is as good as a wink, and Chuykov read this guarded statement as an invitation to keep VI Army in the city by harassing operations. Shumilov put his 64th Army into a small offensive in the southern area, at Beketovka, ostensibly designed to relieve the city, but actually meant to divert German attention from what was going on north of the Don.

What was going on north of the Don certainly needed to be kept from German eyes – if possible. The Stavka team – Army General Zhukov, Colonel-General Vassilevsky – familiar faces, these, at Don Front headquarters had come once again at the beginning of November, bringing with them a new visitor, Colonel-General of Artillery N N Voronov, the Head of Artillery of the Red Army. On November 3rd Zhukov started the final round of

conferences of all commanders down to divisional level, first at the headquarters of 5th Tank Army of the new South-West Front, then one for their Don Front counterparts, and finally one for the commanders of the southern pincer, at HQ Stalingrad Front.

The scope of the plan was vast, and so were the forces assembled to execute it. From west to east along the Don from Veshenskaya to the beginning of the big bend, and from there across to the Volga at Yerzovka stood five armies – 5th Tank, and 21st of South-West Front, 65th, 24th, and 66th of Don Front. To the south the reinforced 57th and 51st Armies of Stalingrad Front had already occupied the defiles between the series of lakes. Altogether the force comprised over one million men, with thirteen thousand five hundred and forty-one guns and mortars, eight hundred and ninety four tanks, and one thousand one hundred and fifteen aircraft. That the Germans had only been dimly aware of its existence, and only too late recognised its purpose was a tribute to Red Army security and skill in deception, and a reproach to the intelligence services of Hitler and his generals, but it must also have contained some element of luck.

Huge though the force was, it was none too big for the task set it. In numbers, it was slightly inferior to the total Axis forces in the area, since these numbered also slightly more than one million, with about ten thousand guns and mortars, six hundred and seventy-five tanks, and about twelve hundred aircraft, and thus it was only in tanks and guns that the Red Army had a clear edge. With this in mind, and in accordance with the good military principle of striking the enemy at his weakest point, Zhukov and his Stavka colleagues planned to concentrate their tanks, guns, and aircraft against the Rumanian forces on either side of VI and IV Panzer Armies – III Rumanian on the Don and IV Rumanian west of the lakes south of Stalingrad.

• These Rumanian armies were known to be poorly equipped, disgruntled (few of them could see what business they had there in the depths of Russia), and often on bad terms with the Germans. Furthermore, because

of the shortage of German troops which had made it necessary to seek a Rumanian contribution, Hitler had had to bow to the wishes of the Rumanian leader, Marshal Antonescu, and employ them as complete formations, against the wishes of some of his generals who wanted to 'corset' them with German troops to stiffen their resistance. Their equipment was lamentably inadequate, particularly in anti-tank weapons and tanks, and to make matters worse VIII Italian Army, on the immediate west of III Rumanian, was in little better case, so there would be little hope of help from the flank if III Rumanian got into trouble.

Because of their inadequate equipment and low level of enthusiasm for the cause, the Rumanians had done nothing about the Soviet bridgeheads on the Don's west bank at Serafimovich and Kletskaya, but they had kept an anxious eye on them, and could not but notice, however strict the Soviet precautions, that they were being reinforced. The Rumanian commander, Colonel-General Dumitrescu, had more than once warned of the danger represented by the Soviet bridgeheads and though he had not gone so far as to volunteer the services of his troops to eliminate them, he had requested the directing of German tank and anti-tank units to III Army's sector.

Hitler did not believe that any serious danger was presented by the Red Army bridgeheads over the Don, and here his normal urge to write off the Russians before events really justified such a course was fortified by a military intelligence assessment, made in September, which credited the Red Army with 'no operational reserves of any significance'. In the light of hindsight, this assessment seems incredible, but at the time it was made the Soviet territories under German occupation contained about 40% of the Soviet Union's total population, the Red Army's losses had already come to more than the entire armed forces strength with which it had started the war, and the use of

Assembly of power. Vast Russian forces —infantry, light armour and squadrons of the many T34s, were brought up for the pincer battles

older reservists, sailors, and men drafted from Siberia gave fair reason to believe that the 'Russian steamroller' was fast running out of steam. Nevertheless, the way in which this assessment, based as it would have to be on inadequate information, 'guesstimation', and approximation, had been elevated by Hitler and OKH into an article of faith, reflects little credit on the headquarters procedures of Germany's armed forces.

Anyway, though Hitler was not too disposed to take the Rumanian anxieties seriously, he did agree to make tank and anti-tank forces available to them, and ordered XLVIII Panzer Corps into III Army's sector on November 10th. The first snows of the winter had already arrived by the time the Corps, temporarily detached from IV Panzer Army, left for Serafimovich, taking with it some units of XIV Panzer Division.

The Corps consisted of XXII German Panzer Division and a Rumanian tank division, and was in bad shape. It had large numbers of obsolete Czech tanks, but few of the better German Mk III and IV tanks; its Panzer Grenadier regiment had been removed from it some months before, and its Assault Engineer battalion had been detached by Paulus for use at Stalingrad. Since September it had been inactive, lying behind Italian VIII Army, and because of the fuel shortage many of the tank engines had not been started for two months, while the tanks had been dug in, and camouflaged and protected against frost with straw and reeds. When the German division was ordered to take the road, sixty-five of its one hundred and four tanks could not be started and even after intensive work only forty-two could be put in running order. The reason was simple. The straw had attracted mice, the mice went into the tanks to look for food, and developed a taste for the insulation covering the electrical wiring, so when the tanks were started up short circuits developed in their electrical systems, and several of them were set on fire by sparks. The other formation – Rumanian I Panzer Divisions – did not suffer this particular problem, but of its one hundred and eight tanks all bar ten were obsolete Czech 38-Ts, no match for the

Soviet T-34s or KV-1s. As XLVIII Panzer Corps slithered and sparked its uncertain way towards its new sector, few of its sweating soldiers can have regarded the episode as a good augury for the coming battle, nor would their spirits have been raised had they known that this crazy collection of vehicles was being placed right in the path of the Soviet armoured spearhead – Lieutenant-General P L Romanenko's 5th Tank Army, a full-strength formation with hundreds of T-34s, the best medium tanks then available to any army in the world.

November opened badly for Germany. On the 4th, Rommel's army in Africa began the long retreat to Tripoli, and on the 8th Anglo-American forces landed in French North Africa. Hitler found it necessary to invade unoccupied France, thus tying up formations which at a pinch could have been despatched to the Eastern Front, whither so many of the German units in Western Europe were later to go. In the midst of the crises thus engendered, and with Army Group B at last beginning to wake up to the danger which hung over it, Hitler left the headquarters at Vinnitsa to go to Munich, as November 9th 1942, was the anniversary of the unsuccessful attempt to seize power in Bavaria in 1923, and he was due to speak at the celebrations in the Burgerbraukeller. What were disaster in Africa and danger on the Eastern Front compared with the opportunity to revive old memories and make a misleading speech on how well the war was going under his inspired leadership, in particular how 'no power on earth will force us out of Stalingrad'?

Back in the city, meantime, Chuykov had a new problem – the ice on the Volga. Because of the immense size of the river, and its relatively southerly position, it can take weeks or even months to ice up. Once the temperature reaches 15° (Centigrade) below zero, large masses of ice move down it, rendering it completely impassable by shipping, though once the temperature drops further, the mass of ice freezes solid and stops moving, making the river usable by wheeled or foot traffic. The large ice mass was now in motion, and Chuykov feared that

Paulus would time another offensive for the period when 62nd Army would be deprived of its supply routes, so he had already done what he could to stock up during the few days of navigation remaining, and had laid down strict orders of priority – first, men and ammunition; second, food; third, warm clothing.

But somehow or other Chuykov could not get the supply services to understand that a cold, hungry soldier with ammunition is better than a warm, well-fed one without. The Deputy Head of Supply Services of the Red Army, General Vinogradov, was in charge on the east bank, and he had his own ideas, so a flood of earflaps and felt boots cascaded upon 62nd Army, until its depots were bulging with surplus clothing and food, and Chuykov had to persuade Khrushchev to intervene and make Vinogradov go away, after which 62nd Army proceeded to beg, borrow, or steal whatever ammunition it could lay its hands on. Former sailors and fishermen in its ranks made their own boats and rafts so that the more orthodox means of delivering ammunition could be supplemented during the few navigation days left. Food was brought over as well, and Chuykov accumulated a reserve of 12 tons of chocolate. At a pinch, the Army could survive on that for one or two weeks.

Patrols confirmed that Paulus was regrouping for a last heave once again, when they established that VI Army's last uncommitted formation – 44th Infantry Division – had been brought into the city. Clearly the German offensive would be soon – Chuykov's fear was that Paulus would co-ordinate it with the interruption of navigation on the river was about to prove fully justified.

At 0630 hours on November 11th, Paulus put in his last bid for capture of the city, with seven divisions (XIV and XXIV Panzer, 100th Light, 44th, 79th, 305th, and 389th Infantry), with elements of 161st and 294th brought in by air from Rossosh and Millerovo. They came in on a three-mile front between Volkhovstroyevskaya Street and the Banny Gully, astonishingly strongly considering that most of them had already been very roughly handled in the fighting of the previous weeks. Chuykov's troops met them head-on, and the isolated northern group under Colonel Gorokhov attempted to relieve the pressure by counterattacking from the railway bridge over the mouth of the Mechetka towards the Tractor Factory.

After five hours of the grim close-quarter fighting which had become the norm for the battle, Paulus committed his tactical reserve, overrunning the right flank of Gorishny's 95th Division and reaching the Volga in the Red October plant area on a frontage of about 600 yards. Lyudnikov's 138th Division was now cut off from the rest of 62nd Army, which had thus been divided into three parts – Gorokhov's northern group in Spartanovka, Lyudnikov's division on the Volga north of the Red October plant, and the main body from south of the latest German breach to the Mamayev Kurgan.

But this time there was not the tension that there had been in 62nd Army on previous critical days, for the defenders knew that this was Paulus' last fling, and though the fighting was hard, the Luftwaffe's support lacked the edge it had had in October, as Richthofen's men were down from 3,000 sorties a day to about a third of that number. The Soviet casualties were very heavy in the fighting on November 11th-12th (118th Guards Regiment had two hundred and fifty men when the fighting began on the 11th, and lost Two hundred and Forty-four of them in the first five and a half hours), but this time everyone could see that there would be an end to it, and soon.

Sure enough, on the evening of the 12th the German attack petered out, though there was still plenty of action and Lyudnikov's division was in a very precarious position. Chuykov took to calling him by radio to tell him that help was on the way. This was pure bluff, and was intended for German ears, in fact Chuykov had no help to give in the short term, and the relief of Lyudnikov's division would be a matter of creeping back towards his positions building by building. Now everywhere in the city 62nd Army began to counterattack, block by block, house by house, room by room. Almost imperceptibly the tide was

Last bid to capture the city. German infantry attack

The Red Army holds

beginning to turn.

On the evening of the 18th Chuykov and his senior officers were holding a rather despondent meeting in their dug-out. They were worried about manpower, as Yeremenko had not kept his promise of draft reinforcements.

The telephone rang. It was Front HQ. 'There will be an Order coming through shortly. Stand by to receive it.'

They looked at each other. What could this be? Suddenly, Gurov, the 'Member of Military Council' struck his forehead. 'I know what it is! It's the order for the big counter-offensive!'

It was. South-West and Don Fronts were to attack the following morning from the Kletskaya area, making for the big Don bridge at Kalach. Stalingrad Front would take the offensive on the 20th from the Raygorod area, also heading for Kalach, while 62nd Army would keep the Germans in the city busy by counterattacks, so that they could not transfer forces to other sectors. Zhukov had baited his trap well. Now he was about to spring it.

Zhukov springs
the trap

For the Germans of VI and IV Panzer Armies, November 19th began like any other day. Ahead of them was the pack-ice still rolling sullenly down the Volga and behind them, the mutely reproachful chimneys of the Stalingrad suburbs rising out of the ruins. As the sky lightened, the usual exchanges of fire began. The morning was a foggy one, and neither their own nor the Soviet air forces were in evidence. They had begun another attack on the previous day, but the zest which had been in evidence a week before was lacking, for the pitcher had been too often to the well, and only their discipline kept them going. It looked as if they would spend the winter whittling away at the tough Ivans of Chuykov's storm groups; it was a far cry from the old war of movement of the summer.

Did they but know it, the war of movement had begun again seventy miles to the north-west of them. At 0730 hours Voronov's guns and mortars – three thousand five hundred of them – laid down an eighty-minute barrage against Rumanian III Army.

The barrage lifted and through the mist there came down on the dazed Rumanians the Soviet infantry, wave upon wave, and with them the menacing shapes of the T-34s, over two hundred of them, in 5th Tank Army brushing aside the Rumanian left wing, while the 4th Tank Corps of Christyakov's 21st Army hammered against its right flank. For a while the Rumanians seemed to be holding, but soon T-34's broke through and mixed formations of tanks and cavalry plunged into the rear areas of III Army, shooting up headquarters, shattering the reserve units as they attempted to move up, overtaking and scattering the front line infantry as it attempted to withdraw.

The Rumanians broke, and their divisions fell to pieces, streaming in panic towards the rear. Behind them the stolid Soviet infantry plodded on, rounding up the pathetic groups of fleeing Rumanians, while the mobile forces gathered themselves for their next missions – 1st Tank Corps to head south-east towards the Don, 26th Tank Corps towards Kalach and its

Captive in the mist

Left: Briefing before battle
Left below: Armour moves up
Above: Katyusha rocket batteries signal the beginning of the artillery barrage

bridge, 4th Tank Corps towards Golubinsky; all in fact heading for the rear of VI Army, with nothing in their way except the rickety XLVIII Panzer Corps with its mouse-nibbled tanks. First it was ordered north-east against 4th Tank Corps, but as soon as it was on the road it was ordered to turn about and head north-west against the much larger and more dangerous force, the two corps (1st and 26th) of 5th Tank Army.

The XLVIII Corps did its best, but the mice had done their work too well and the unlucky crews had another difficulty to contend with: they had had no snow-sleeves for the tank-tracks, so those that could move at all slithered desperately over the frozen steppes. They managed to get across the path of Romanenko's tanks and to do some damage, but they were twenty against over ten times that number, and 5th Tank Army was in a hurry. It wheeled left and right round the obstruction, accepted the loss of ten per cent of its tanks as fortune of war, and roared off to the south-east, barely pausing in its stride. By dawn on the 29th the 26th Tank Corps was in the village of Perelazovsky, and the headquarters of V Rumanian Army Corps was smashed. The 5th Tank Army had been given four days to get to Kalach, and already had covered more than one-third of the way.

Dawn on the 29th saw the beginning of Yeremenko's attack, towards Kalach from the south, with 51st Army, and towards the rear of VI Army at Stalingrad from the south-east with 57th Army. Here, too, the Rumanian-held sectors had been chosen as targets for Soviet onslaught. Yeremenko had the smaller force, two armies as against the five in the north, and he had not received command of the northern force for which he had longed those long weeks ago in Moscow, but still, he was commanding a major attack, and, as he wrote later, 'there was nothing more pleasing for those who had known the bitterness of retreat and the bloody labour of many months of defence.'

Yeremenko's attack was itself a two-pronged one. On his right, parts of 64th and 57th Armies with a force of six infantry divisions would strike up towards the rear of VI Army, and when they had made a breach the 13th Mechanised Corps would advance towards the Chervlenaya river to pen in the Stalingrad force, while on his left 51st Army would make a hole through which the 4th Mechanised and 4th Cavalry Corps would be launched towards Sovetsky and on to Kalach, thus to forge the ring of encirclement around the bulk of Army Group B. The forces facing Yeremenko's assault grouping comprised the VI Army Corps of Rumanian IV Army, with four infantry divisions and cavalry, stiffened somewhat by the German XXIX Motorised Division.

Here too there was thick mist, and the attack, scheduled for 0800 hours had to be postponed first until 0900 then until 1000 hours. Finally the mist began to lift, and at 1000 *Katyusha* salvoes signalled the beginning of the artillery bombardment. By 1500 the Axis defences had been pierced on all sectors and the mobile forces were away in full cry over the horizon.

The key to success of the operation was of course the advance on Kalach by the tanks and cavalry. But these by themselves could create only a token encirclement, which would have to be turned into a real one by substantial forces of infantry, so the Soviet plan of attack on the northern sector, where Zhukov had personally taken charge, included a number of secondary attacks, some aimed at fragmenting the Axis forces in the area, others at creating an 'outer front of encirclement' which meant establishing forces in positions from which they would be able to withstand any attempt to relieve Paulus' force once it was surrounded. Thus while Romanenko's Tank Corps were heading south-east towards Kalach, his infantry was making south-west and south to establish itself along the east bank of the River Chir, and the 65th and 24th Armies of Rokossovsky's Don Front were pinning down the German divisions in the small bend of the Don, while his remaining army (66th) kept the north flank of VI Army busy in the corridor between Don and Volga.

Army Group B had had some inkling (though too late and too indefinite) of the coup being prepared along the north flank of its front, but Yeremenko's attack south of Stalingrad took them completely by surprise, and the only German formation of any size in the southern area was the XXIX Motorised Division, commanded by Major-General Leyser. Like XLVIII Panzer Corps in the north it was bedevilled by conflicting orders and hampered by fleeing Rumanians, but at least the mice had not been at its tanks. On the morning of November 20th the commander of IV Panzer-Army, Colonel-General Hoth, dispatched the division to seal off the breach made by the mixed force from Soviet 57th and 64th Armies, and in the course of the morning it inflicted a severe local reverse on XIII Mechanised Corps, temporarily halting the Soviet advance.

While the action was still in progress, Hoth received news that the Rumanian front had been broken by Soviet 51st Army further south, and he prepared to send the division down to deal with this, too. Meanwhile the commander of the Soviet mobile force, 4th Mechanised Corps, heard of the serious reverse suffered by his colleagues further north, and on reaching the Zety area he stopped, expecting to fight a defensive battle. Since his was the southern prong of the pincer movement on Kalach, there was some danger that the entire operation would stall, but in fact XXIX Motorised was ordered back to the Stalingrad area to defend the southern flank of the position there, as despite the temporary setback to XIII Mechanised Corps it had proved relatively easy to get the offensive going again.

Yeremenko's only remaining problem was how to get 4th Mechanised Corps on the move once more, and he solved this by despatching an aircraft to the Corps Commander, General Volsky, with a 'categorical demand' to get on with the job. Volsky complied, and gave no further trouble, resuming his advance on the 22nd and reaching Kalach twenty-four hours later. His Corps' performance, in fact, earned it elevation to 'Guards'.

The slow reaction of the Germans to the cataclysms on VI Army's flanks requires explanation, as the German army after all prided itself, not without reason, on the excellence of its staff work and the speed with which it could react to situations. All autumn VI Army had tempted fate by concentrating so much of its weight forward and underestimating the Soviet ability to exploit the fact. Germany had already that month been hit by a number of crises in other theatres, and it might have been thought that its leaders would be at their posts, working day and night to find an answer to the problems so suddenly heaped upon them.

Not a bit of it! Hitler, after the Munich celebration, had gone to his mountain retreat at Berchtesgaden in the Bavarian Alps. HQ Area 1, the relevant section of OKW, was in makeshift quarters on the edge of the town, and the operations staff of OKW was in its special train in the station at Salzburg, a few miles away over the Austrian border, while OKH was hundreds of miles off, in the East Prussian forests near Angerburg. The Luftwaffe High Command (OKL) was also

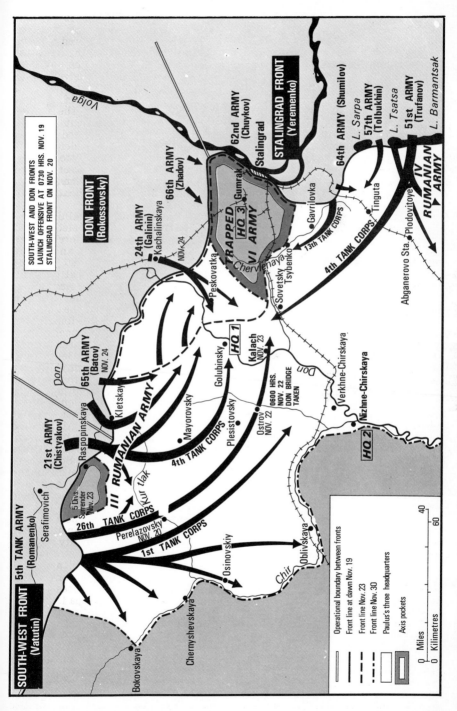

SOUTH-WEST AND DON FRONTS
LAUNCH OFFENSIVE AT 0730 HRS. NOV. 19
STALINGRAD FRONT ON NOV. 20

DON FRONT (Rokossovsky)

STALINGRAD FRONT (Yeremenko)

62nd ARMY (Chuykov)

Stalingrad

66th ARMY (Zhadov)

24th ARMY (Galinin)

Kachalinskaya

NOV. 24

Peskovatka

TRAPPED [HQ 3] VI ARMY

Gumrak

Chervlenaya

Gavrilovka

64th ARMY (Shumilov)

L. Sarpa

57th ARMY (Tolbukhin)

L. Tsatsa

51st ARMY (Trufanov)

L. Barmantsak

IV RUMANIAN ARMY

Plodovitoye

Tinguta

13th TANK CORPS

4th TANK CORPS

Abganerovo Sta.

Sovetsky

Tsybenko

65th ARMY (Batov)
NOV. 24

[HQ 1]

Kalach
NOV. 23

Golubinsky

0600 HRS.
NOV. 23
DON BRIDGE
TAKEN

Verkhne-Chirskaya

Nizhne-Chirskaya

Kletskaya

Ostrov
NOV. 22

[HQ 2]

21st ARMY (Chistyakov)

Raspopinskaya

Don

Mayorovsky

Plesistovsky

5 Divs.
Surrender
Nov. 23

III RUMANIAN ARMY

4th TANK CORPS

Kurtlak

26th   TANK CORPS

Perelazovsky
NOV. 20

1st TANK CORPS

Osinovskiy

Obllivskaya

Chir

SOUTH-WEST FRONT (Vatutin)

5th TANK ARMY (Romanenko)

Serafimovich

Chernyshevskaya

Bokovskaya

Volga

Operational boundary between fronts
Front line at dawn Nov. 19
Front line Nov. 23
Front line Nov. 30
Paulus's three headquarters
Axis pockets

0   40   Miles
0   60   Kilometres

123

up there, though as usual no-one was quite sure where the Reichsmarshall and C-in-C of the Luftwaffe, Hermann Goring, might be (it turned out he was in Paris). To make matters even more complicated, VI Army headquarters were also on the move. Up to the opening of the Soviet counter-offensive they had been at Golubinsky, west of the Don, but a permanent headquarters had been built at Nizhne-Chirskaya, some forty miles further down the Don, at its junction with the Chir.

It was intended to serve as HQ VI Army during the coming winter, and had excellent communications to HQ Army Group B, OKH, and OKW. When therefore, the headquarters at Golubinsky were threatened by the advance of Romanenko's tanks, and even more closely by the forward movement of the 4th Tank Corps operating in front of Chistyakov's 21st Army, the Golubinsky headquarters were hastily evacuated on November 21st, and a wild rush through the night ended in arrival at Nizhe-Chirskaya, on the morning of November 22nd. Paulus claimed that he had gone to Nizhne-Chirskaya to make use of its excellent communications facilities and acquaint himself with the situation before moving his headquarters back into the pocket which was forming, but Hitler, on the other hand, assumed he was leaving his troops in the lurch, and at once ordered him to take up headquarters at the Gumrak airfield on the outskirts of Stalingrad.

Whatever the truth of the matter, VI Army lacked leadership during the vital days of November 21st-23rd, while the Soviet forces moved with inexorable speed over the 125-mile gap between Romanenko's and Yeremenko's start lines. At a time when speed and co-ordination were essential if anything was to be saved from the wreck, Paulus and his staff were trundling up and down the icy roads of the Don steppe – it is just slightly odd that Paulus had taken so many of his staff to Nizhne-Chirskaya if all he wanted to do there was make a few telephone calls, but every commander has his own methods.

Not that Paulus had been completely inert. In Stalingrad itself, on orders from Weichs at Army Group HQ, he

had terminated all attacks, and pulled out elements of XIV, XVI and XXIV Panzer divisions for despatch to the Don against the advancing columns of South-West and Don Fronts, and on the afternoon of the 22nd he and his Chief of Staff, Major-General Schmidt, flew into Gumrak to the new headquarters.

Events were now moving almost too quickly to follow. Everywhere the Rumanian front had crumbled, and the Soviet strike forces were moving fast through open snow-covered country on both sides of the Don. If they were to establish a really solid encirclement one force or other must get across the river, which was, of course, frozen, but would not bear the weight of tanks and heavy guns. There was only one bridge – at Kalach – and the problem was whether it could be seized before the Germans could blow it up. An orthodox attack would be no good, as the demolition charges were already in place, and the only hope was swift *coup de main*, before the bridge guard could be aware what was happening.

Major-General Rodin's 26th Tank Corps seized the village of Ostrov on the night of November 21st-22nd, from where Kalach was about three hours' run down the road for a mobile column, if it could get through without arousing suspicion, so he decided it was worth a try, and assembled a column of five tanks, two companies of infantrymen in lorries, and one armoured car. In charge of the column was the commander of 14th Motorised Rifle Brigade, Lieutenant-Colonel G N Filippov. The column drew up on the Ostrov-Kalach road, ready to go, at 0300 hours and Filippov climbed into the leading vehicle. 'Lights on', he ordered. They were going to pretend to be Germans. Surely the bridge guards would not expect a Soviet column to approach the bridge, with no attempt at concealment, and its headlights blazing?

The next three hours were a time of almost unbearable suspense as the rest of Rodin's force made ready to follow up and waited for news. Just before 0600 hours, Filippov's men

Now speed was essential as the Russian infantry flooded across the Don Steppe

125

Stormoviks over the battlefield

approached the bridge, and part of the detachment hived off to seize the near side when the signal was given, while the rest rolled on to the bridge and disappeared into the darkness. A few minutes later a rocket soared into the air from the far bank. They had made it; the bridge was in Soviet hands and intact. Not content with this, the detachment then attempted to capture the town itself, but this was overambitious for two companies and five tanks. The Germans, now thoroughly aroused, pushed them back, surrounded them and endeavoured to recapture the bridge. Filippov's small force was under heavy pressure for many hours, but finally Rodin's main force arrived to relieve it and prepared to take the town.

While the Tank Corps were on the rampage, the infantry were tightening their grip on the pockets of by-passed Rumanians in the north. The Rumanian IV and V Corps, surrounded at the Village of Raspopinskaya, provided the first major haul of prisoners, when towards evening on the 23rd the officer in command, Brigadier Stanescu sent an officer out with a white flag to discuss surrender terms. On receiving satisfactory conditions, his force of five divisions capitulated, and twenty-seven thousand officers and men trudged off into captivity.

The afternoon of the 23rd also saw a much more important development than the mere rounding up of the Raspopinskaya group, significant though that was, when at 1600 hours the forward elements of Volsky's corps, which had captured the farm buildings at Sovetsky, saw tanks approaching from the north. For a time it was difficult to make out whose they were, but as they came nearer the familiar squat silhouettes were unmistakable. They were T-34s of General Kravchenko's 4th Tank Corps, spearheading the advance of South-West Front from Kalach.

The door had been closed behind VI and IV Panzer Armies, and all that remained was to bolt it. That, too, came nearer to completion that day, for in the evening the forward infantry units of 21st Army reached the Don near Kalach – the town itself having fallen to a joint attack by two of Romanko's tank brigades just before 1400 hours. The full extent of their success was as yet unknown even to the Stavka, which believed they had about eighty five thousand Axis troops encircled, whereas in actual fact there were inside the ring twenty German and two Rumanian divisions, plus large numbers of individual and specialist units, a total of about three hundred and thirty thousand men.

This was the true measure of 62nd Army's achievement: by holding on to Stalingrad they had drawn more and more German troops into the area, and prepared the ground for a *coup* of epic dimensions. They had withstood tremendous pressure, and now the roles were to be reversed, for the besiegers had become the besieged, and the encircled Germans, Rumanians, and Croats were to suffer all that 62nd Army had suffered, for longer, and with the added burdens of cold, hunger, and hopelessness, for unlike 62nd Army they were not defending a cherished piece of their homeland, on the banks of a river which to a Russian is just as much 'liquid history' as the Thames to an Englishman.

They were the soldiers of an army of conquest, an army whose performance depended on a conviction of professional superiority, just as much as the ideology of its political masters depended on a theory of racial dominance. Discipline and the fear of captivity in the hands of the *Untermensch* would keep them at their posts, but the time would come when the *possibility* of death in a Soviet prison camp would seem infinitely preferable to the *certainty* of death from cold, starvation, sickness, or a Russian bullet.

Twenty-seven thousand Rumanian officers and men trudged off into captivity

'VI army will still be in position at Easter'

At first the German reactions to encirclement were mixed. Some of the subordinate commanders felt that Stalingrad should be evacuated at once, while it was still possible to break through to the West. Others were reluctant to give up the positions at Stalingrad, not merely because of the effort which had been put into gaining them, but because the cellars and ruins at least offered shelter from the vicious Russian winter. In any case, whatever the ultimate decision would be, everyone could agree on the need to defend the Army's rear. This was an essential prerequisite to any future action, as clearly there would be neither breakout nor holding on if the Red Army overran the German positions from behind.

For the moment, therefore, Weichs had hedged his bets, and with the possibility of encirclement in mind, he had already on November 21st issued an order to VI Army to hold Stalingrad and the front along the Volga 'in any circumstances' *and* to prepare to break out. But before there could be any thought of a breakout, a number of problems would have to be solved, and the most important of these was fuel. Because of the general shortage of fuel, all German formations were under-supplied, and priority was given to those with mobile tasks to perform. Since September, VI Army and its accompanying formations from IV Panzer Army had been engaged relatively low requirements in fuel and therefore with low allocations.

Ammunition was also short, and Paulus estimated that he had food for six days only. He therefore radioed to Army Group B on the evening of the 22nd, stating that he intended holding Stalingrad, but that he could not do so unless he succeeded in sealing off his front to the south and could receive plentiful air supply, and requested freedom of action to abandon his northern front and Stalingrad in order to break out if necessary. The reply to this request came almost at once, and not from Wechs but from Hitler himself. The VI Army must stay put and 'must know that I am doing everything necessary to assist and relieve it. I shall issue my orders in good time.'

Now VI Army was defending . . . and
winter was coming

131

Paulus tried again on the morning of the 23rd, and Weichs supported his request by emphasising to OKH the impossibility of adequate air supply. Even before a reply was received, Paulus held a conference with his Corps Commanders, and just before midnight despatched a message to Hitler personally, pointing out the deterioration in the conditions at the front since the previous day. Soviet breakthroughs in south and south-west were imminent, many of the field and anti-tank artillery batteries had no ammunition left, and the army faced 'annihilation in the immediate future' unless abandonment of the eastern and northern fronts, with concentration of all forces for a break-out to south and south-west (along the east bank of the Don towards Rostov) was authorised. Even so, much material would have to be abandoned, but some of it, and the majority of the men, would be saved. Again he asked for freedom of action.

Hitler's reply arrived the next morning in the form of a *Fuhrer-befehl* (a Fuhrer's Order, the most binding form of command). Not only was there to be no withdrawal, but all units of VI Army still west of the Don were to withdrew eastwards: *into* the pocket. The order ended with the words 'The present Volga and present Northern Fronts to be held at all costs. Supplies coming by air'.

The question of air supply was crucial to Hitler's decision, and requires closer examination. It has already been mentioned that the Soviet commanders thought that there were about eighty-five thousand Axis troops in the pocket, whereas there were actually about three hundred and thirty thousand. This figure was only established after the battle, and at the time the question of air supply arose, the Germans themselves were extremely uncertain how many men would have to be supplied. The Operations Staff thought there were about four hundred thousand; the Army Quartermaster General, Wagner, made it three hundred thousand; about two hundred thousand under command.

Thus the discussion over aircraft requirements took place in an atmosphere of great uncertainty, and the figures eventually reached were approximate only. It was eventually decided on the basis of General Wagner's figures that about six hundred tons a day would be needed, and that to supply this amount about three hundred of the Luftwaffe's work-horses, the three-engined Junkers 52, would be necessary. It was fairly clear from the beginning that these air-craft were not to be had; the minimum figure of three hundred could not be attained, let alone the margins needed to cover aircraft under repair, damaged on take-off or landing on the improvised airfields, or shot down by the Soviet fighters and anti-aircraft, which would raise the numbers required to at least five hundred.

In the circumstances the Chief-of-Staff of the Air Force, Colonel-General Jeschonnek, placed so many reservations on the possibility of air supply that it was clear he doubted its feasibility. Göring, however, disregarded the caution of his advisers, and with a flamboyant contempt for the possible undertook that the Luftwaffe would keep VI Army supplied from the air. This was what Hitler wanted to hear, and he ordered Stalingrad to be held, in the hope that somehow or other Göring would cajole a miracle out of the Luftwaffe. At the same time Hitler was hopeful that the Soviet recovery could be wished out of existence by the exercise of superior generalship, and the man he selected on November 20th to restore the situation was the conqueror of the Crimea, Field-Marshal Erich von Manstein, who had already shown himself in the French and Russian campaigns to be of outstanding talent, and was at present serving on the northern sector of the Front.

He was instructed by OKH to form a new Army Group in the Don bend, between Army Groups A and B, taking under command VI, IV Panzer, and III Rumanian Armies, with the task of 'bringing the enemy attacks to a standstill and recapturing the positions previously occupied by us.' Considering that two of the three, armies were already almost encircled and the third being battered to a pulp by the Soviet armour, it was a not immodest requirement to lay upon a general even of Manstein's

quality.

Manstein and his staff had to travel by train because of the weather conditions and the uncertainties of rail travel in Russian conditions (railway lines were a favourite target for the growing numbers of Soviet partisans) and it was the 24th before he reached the headquarters of Army Group B at Starobelsk where he found Weichs and his Chief-of-Staff, von Sodenstern in a state of apathetic despondency. He was unable to establish even whether VI Army had received the instruction despatched by him before he began the journey, to keep control of the Kalach bridge at whatever cost, but in any case, it mattered little, as they had lost it two days before, and by the time Manstein reached Novocherkassk, where his headquarters were to be, he had in effect no forces left.

Five of the seven divisions of III

Left: Field-Marshal Eric von Manstein
Below: The Luftwaffe, Göring boasted, would now keep VI Army supplied

Rumanian Army had been swept up in
the Raspopinskaya surrender, and
though the encircled armies at Stalingrad were still in being, their freedom
of action was so restricted by the
Fuhrerbefehl of two days previously
that there was little he could do with
them. Worse still, Zhukov had not
been idle while Manstein's train was
creeping across Russia. He had been
pouring infantry across the Don to
establish firm fronts facing both
west and east against either a sortie
to relieve VI Army or an attempt by
it to break out. They were heavily
supported by artillery and *Katyushas*,
including over thousand anti-tank
guns'.

No brilliant improvisation would
help here; what Manstein needed was
force. To complicate his task, he
credited the Russians with the intention to strike right down to the south
coast at Rostov, thus cutting off
Army Group A as well, whereas in
fact, though this was a task given to
Vatutin and Yeremenko for a later
phase of the operation, it was entirely
secondary to the destruction of the
Stalingrad force, and received lower
priority both in force and supply so
that Yeremenko was unable to carry
it out. This was a problem that would
face Manstein only later, and the
breathing space given to him by this
was to be well exploited.

While the front of Army Group Don
was held by a mixture of units formed
ad hoc from supply personnel, Luftwaffe ground staff, and men returning
from leave, Manstein bombarded OKH
with requests for forces, and during
the first days of December these
began arriving, XI Panzer from OKH
Reserve, VI Panzer from Western
Europe, 62nd, 294th, and 336th Infantry
two Luftwaffe Field Divisions, and
one of mountain troops. What was
left of XLVIII Panzer Corps was also
brought into the line, and when it
became apparanet that Zhokov did
not for the moment contemplate any
major attack across the Chir, but
intended his force there to hold the
ring while the seven field armies
which he had concentrated around
Stalingrad got on with the job of
annihilating VI Army, everyone could
breathe more freely.

The forces on the Chir, now grouped

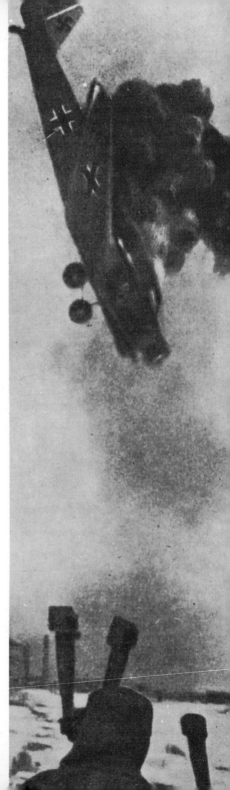

into 'Army Detachment Hollidt' (its commander) even succeeded in holding their bridgehead at Nizhne-Chirskaya, a mere twenty-five miles from the western perimeter of VI Army. Soviet attempts to eliminate it and to make some crossings of their own were frustrated by XI Panzer in the second week of December in a series of brilliantly conducted actions which for the time being eliminated the threat of further Soviet penetration across the Chir, though at the expense of about half the divisions' tanks, and enabled Army Group Don to concentrate on the relief operation, while divisions continued to arrive from the Caucasus, northern sectors of the front, Poland, and the West.

Although the bridgehead at Nizhne-Chirskaya was relatively near to the Stalingrad force (twenty-five miles), Manstein decided not to mount the main relief attempt from there, as it was too obvious a choice, and in that

Left and below: **Russian ack-ack closes the ring**

sector it would be easy for the Russians to reinforce their cordon. In addition, to make the attempt from there would involve an opposed crossing of the Don, so he chose instead to approach from the south-west, though the distance involved was seventy-five miles. Here Yeremenko's troops were more thinly spread, and would take longer to reinforce, while instead of the Don only the minor Aksay and Myshkova rivers would have to be forced.

Under the plan, code-named *Wintergewitter* (Winter Tempest), the relief force, headed by Colonel-General Hoth and the staff of IV Panzer Army (now unemployed because most of the army itself was inside the pocket) could either make straight for Stalingrad or, if the Soviet resistance proved too strong, could thrust north along the east bank of the Don to the Nizhne-Chirskaya bridgehead, where XLVIII Panzer Corps would join them for a thrust along the short route to the city. Whichever variant of the

135

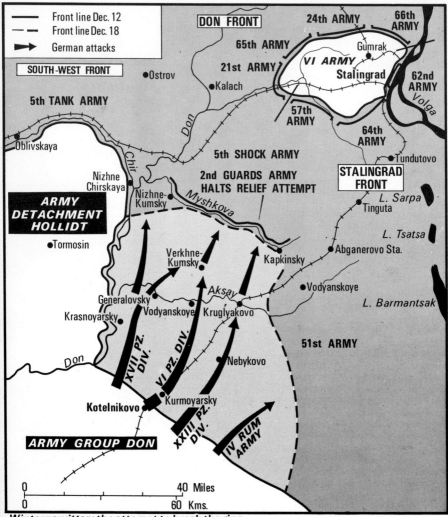

Wintergewitter: the attempt to break the ring

plan was followed, VI Army was to break out and advance to meet the relieving force on receipt of the codeword *Donnerschlag* (Thunderclap).

Donnerschlag presented a difficulty in that it was extremely unlikely that VI Army would be able to hold its existing positions (which it was under a strict injunction from Hitler to do) as well as break out towards the Hoth Group, but this was glossed over in Manstein's operational order so that Hitler's attention would not be drawn to it; in fact he was preparing to face

the Fuhrer with a *fait accompli*, by relieving VI Army and then withdrawing it from its exposed position.

The collection of forces for *Wintergewitter* took some time. The 57th Panzer Corps was extracted from Army Group A, which was very reluctant to give it up, and had considerable trouble with muddy roads while moving back to entrain at Maykop, as the thaw had set in early in the Caucasus. When it arrived, there were found to be insufficient flat-cars for its tanks, some of which,

Mobile light artillery moves up to
support the counterattack

and all of the heavy artillery, had to
be left behind. OKW showed great
unwillingness to release from reserve
XVII Panzer Division, and it eventually arrived ten days late. Nevertheless, a force of thirteen divisions,
including VI, XVII, and XXIII Panzer
was eventually got together, and
Manstein, deciding he could postpone
the attempt no longer sent it off on
December 12th. Behind it a mass of
lorries, tractors and buses waited,
ready to rush three thousand tons of
supplies down the corridor to VI Army,
as soon as Hoth's tanks had opened
the road.

At first the Soviet opposition was
light. The 51st Army consisted of eight
divisions, supported by the 4th
Mechanised Corps, and was manifestly
not strong enough to stop the German
advance, though it could and did
attempt to delay it. The delay was in
itself important, because the real
effort to stop Hoth was to be made on
the Myshkova river between Verkhne-
Kumsky and Kapkinsky, and the force

chosen for the assignment had to be
transported to the area.

The reason for this was that
the second phase of the Soviet offensive (Operation 'Saturn') had been
launched away to the north, where a
strike force provided by Vatutin's
South-West Front and the adjacent
Voronezh Front of General Golikov
(recently promoted after having acted
as Yeremenko's deputy at Stalingrad)
was launched against Italian VIII
Army on the middle Don, after which
it was to bear down on the German
forces along the Chir, smash them and
make down towards Millerovo and
Rostov, behind Army Groups A and
Don.

That which Manstein had feared was
indeed in the mind of Stavka, but
not in the form of Yeremenko's
advance down the Don (though that
too had been planned). The 2nd Guards
Army, commanded by Lieutenant-
General R Y Malinovsky, had been
formed to take part in this offensive,
and was designated to start from
Kalach headed for Rostov and Tagan-
rog, but when it became clear that the
Hoth offensive was a serious under-

137

taking with some chance of success, it was decided to transfer 2nd Guards Army to the Myshkova river.

The army was fresh, not worn down by previous battles, and comprised six full-strength rifle divisions, a mechanised corps, and specialist units. There was one tank regiment in each of the two infantry corps (of three divisions each), and it was, as a Guards formation, better supplied with artillery, machine guns and automatic weapons than the general run of Soviet armies. Many of its men had been transferred from the Navy, and they provided a solid backbone to the divisions. Altogether it was a formidable acquisition of strength, and the only question was whether it could get to the Myshkova before Hoth. It was not a motorised army, so its infantry would have to march the whole way, in the capricious alternation between night frost and daily thaw of the early Russian winter, anything up to one hundred and twenty-five miles.

The offensive by South-West and Voronezh Fronts was launched without the 2nd Guards, and soon began to affect the battle further south. The Italians were soon shattered and the Soviet assault groups began to lever Army Detachment Hollidt out of its positions on the west bank of the Chir, including the Nizhne-Chirskaya bridgehead. This meant that there would be no possibility of assistance from XLVIII Panzer Corps, and the option of an advance up the east bank of the Don no longer existed; now it was the direct thrust or nothing. As against this, Manstein was able on December 17th to commit XVII Panzer on the left wing of the Hoth Group, thus significantly increasing the strength of his mobile force.

This gave Manstein a considerable preponderance in armour over the Soviet forces opposing him, though to continue with the operation was risky while the front north and west of Hoth's group showed every sign of impending collapse. But to abandon the attempt meant to write off the whole of VI Army, because the collapse of the front on the Chir threatened the supply airfields. The airlift had come nowhere near fulfilling Goring's boasts, but without it VI Army could

last only a matter of days, so the breakthrough had become a matter of the utmost urgency.

But, oddly, Paulus was showing little enthusiasm for it now. It seemed he was happy to wait for Hoth to blast a way through to him, and the likelihood that Hoth would be able to do so was hourly growing less, as 2nd Guards Army's forward elements were beginning to deploy along the Myshkova, the smaller Soviet units already there had been put under Malinovsky's command, and a new armoured formation – 7th Tank Corps – had also arrived, under an energetic commander who was already making a name for himself as a tank leader, General P A Rotmistrov. Falling back into line on 2nd Guards Army's right was another Soviet formation, roughly handled already, but still capable of fighting – the 5th Shock Army of General M M Popov. Hoth had lost the race against the Red Army.

The only way to save the operation was for VI Army to break out into the rear of the Soviet forces on the Myshkova, so Manstein contacted Paulus, who was evasive, then got in touch with Zeitzler at OKH asking him to 'take immediate steps to initiate the break-out by VI Army towards IV Panzer Army' – asking him, in effect, to order Paulus to break out, or at least to persuade Hitler to change the order which tied VI Army down in the city. That produced no response either, so having spent much of December 18th in vain attempts to solve the problem by telephone and radio, he decided to try a more personal approach, and that evening he dispatched his Chief Intelligence Officer, Major Eismann, into the pocket, to give Paulus an exposition of his views.

Eismann drove from Novocherkassk to the Morozovskaya airfield and took off from there shortly before dawn, landing at Gumrak at 0750 hours on the 19th. He was at once taken to Army HQ nearby. After he had put Manstein's case for a break-out, Paulus proceeded to emphasise the difficulties of carrying it out. The Chief of Operations and the Quartermaster-General of the Army echoed him, but both expressed the personal opinion that an immediate breakout was not only imperative but feasible.

It was, however, the Chief-of-Staff, Major-General Arthur Schmidt, who gave the definitive answer. He was a convinced Nazi and a strong character who as the siege went on became more and more the real commander of VI Army. 'It is quite impossible to break out just now . . . VI Army will still be in position at Easter. All you people have to do is supply it better.' Eismann argued with them all day, but to no effect, Paulus eventually quoting the *Fuhrerbefehl* as excluding the possibility of a breakout.

When Eismann returned late on the 19th, Manstein toyed with the idea of dismissing Paulus and Schmidt, but the possibility of obtaining approval from OKH and Hitler without long negotiation seemed so low that he gave it up. On the 20th he again attempted to induce Zeitzler to bring pressure to bear, but without result, and finally at 1800 hours he ordered Paulus to 'begin *Wintergewitter* attack

'VI Army will still be in position at Easter . . .'

as soon as possible', emphasising 'It is essential that *Donnerschlag* should immediately follow *Wintergewitter* attack.'

Paulus' only response was a verbal bombardment. To regroup for the attack, he said, would take six days and entail serious risks in the north and west of the perimeter. The troops were too weak, and since they had had to slaughter the horses for food, their mobility was too low for such an undertaking, especially in extreme cold. Manstein rejected all these excuses, and Paulus came back with the final one that it was impossible to comply with the order because it involved an advance of thirty miles and he had fuel for only twenty. In other words, he would not move.

Since Paulus pleaded technical difficulties, and Zeitzler had proven a broken reed, Manstein made one last attempt, a personal appeal to Hitler. On the afternoon of the 21st he telephoned the Führer to try to persuade him that VI Army must break out at once. All Hitler did was to quote Paulus' objections back to him.

Whichever way the Germans tried to move, Russian infantry or Russian armour waited to block them

'Paulus has only enough petrol for fifteen to twenty miles at most. He himself says he can't break out at present'.

Thus was sealed the fate of VI Army. The Army Commander pleaded lack of fuel and the Führer's order. The Führer refused to change the order because the Army Commander pleaded lack of fuel. The blind led the blind into the abyss.

On the Myshkova Hoth, then as in the autumn of 1941 old-fashioned enough to believe that Army Group commander's orders were meant to be carried out, had been locked in battle for several days with Malinovsky's forces. He had managed to get across the river in one place near Nizhne-Kumsky and had surrounded several units of up to a regiment in size. His men were fighting with the characteristic efficiency of the German soldier, though with little hope of success. A dispatch rider who was captured and taken to 2nd Guards Army's Chief of Staff, General Biryuzov, told him 'Our soldiers consider themselves sentenced to death . . .

At its nearest point, the Hoth group was a mere twenty-two miles from VI Army's perimeter, where the soldiers of the beleaguered army could see the flashes of the guns lighting up the night sky away to the south, and hear, when the wind was in the right direction, the rumble of explosions, so their spirits were high in the days before Christmas. On the 22nd Hoth made his final effort, hurling over sixty of his tanks against one regiment of the 24th Guards Rifle Division on Malinovsky's right flank.

The regiment consisted largely of ex-sailors from the Pacific Fleet, who as if to show their contempt for the 'mild' winter of European Russia, cast off their tunics and fought in the sub-zero temperatures in their naval vests. After hours of fighting, Hoth's tanks had to give them best and withdraw. Darkness fell, and in his command post Malinovsky summed up the day's results. 'Today we have finally halted the formidable enemy. Now we'll go into the attack ourselves'.

On Christmas Eve, 2nd Guards Army did just that. Hoth fought a series of stubborn rearguard actions all the way back to his starting line at Kotelnikovo, but by the time the retreat stopped he had been pushed back sixty miles beyond it. On VI Army's southern perimeter they watched night after night as the flashes in the sky receded further and further till finally they were seen no more. On the Chir, too, where the men on the western edge of the Stalingrad perimeter had watched the firework displays from the Nizhne-Chirskaya bridgehead twenty-five miles away, the sky grew dark, and with it the prospects of VI Army.

On New Year's Eve Biryuzov was working in 2nd Guards Army HQ when an officer was ushered in from Rotmistrov, bearing an invitation to a New Year Party. The Chief-of-Staff was a rather grim and solemn man, and his first reaction was that this was an impermissible frivolity. However he thought better of it, and shortly before midnight made his way to the tank general's headquarters in Kotelnikovo. On the way he passed a burnt-out German tank, and impelled by curiosity he shone his torch on it. It was camouflaged for the desert – one of the reinforcements intended for Rommel in Africa. Shrugging his shoulders - he had no love for the Anglo-Americans - he passed on his way.

Opening the door of Rotmistrov's HQ he stopped in amazement. There were all the senior officers, right up to the Chief-of-General Staff, Vasilevsky, standing round a Christmas tree, and on a table nearby all kinds of fruit, wines from France, cheese from Holland, butter and bacon from Denmark, all sorts of conserves from Norway; and all stamped 'For Germans Only'. 'Not all my men can read German', said Rotmistrov' so because of their lack of education they grabbed it all. But we'll have to give the candles back to Hitler so that he can light them in mourning for VI Army'.

A few days before, VI Army too had had a special feast – Christmas Dinner. Six ounces of bread, three of meat paste, one of butter, one of coffee. For Boxing Day there was an extra treat; two horsemeat rissoles per man.

Annihilation

In Stalingrad the cold grew more and more intense. The 62nd Army, from being a beleaguered outpost, was now part of a ring of steel, formed by seven armies. Apart from its old comrades in arms of 64th Army there was 21st, 24th, 57th, 65th, and 66th, all waiting to go in and finish off the quarry. Chuykov still had his problems, of course, since for weeks the masses of ice had come rolling and tumbling down the Volga, and supply had been almost impossible. They had even resorted to air drops by the little PE-2 'sewing machines', but this was very chancy; one hundred yards out in one direction and the Germans got the supplies; one hundred yards the other way and they disappeared into the Volga.

On December 16th, at about 1600 hours, his attention was drawn by a loud crashing noise. Rushing out of his dug-out he saw an immense mass of ice coming down from behind Zaytsevsky Island, crushing everything in its path. It was visibly slowing down, and right opposite the dug-out it came to a halt. The Volga at last was frozen solid, and by next

morning plank roads had been laid cross it so that supplies could now come in with relative ease, new men could come in, and the worst battered divisions could be withdrawn to rest and make up to strength again.

Contact could be made with Lyudnikov's isolated division, and on December 23rd this was done. The next day Sologub's, Smekhotvorov's, and Zholudev's skeletal divisions and the remnants of two infantry brigades were transferred to the reserve to reform, and even as they were leaving, Guryev's began to clear the enfeebled Germans out of the 'Red October' factory. The Mamayev Kurgan was stormed, but the Germans would not be dislodged, and in defence showed that they had learnt well the lessons taught them by 62nd Army.

Despite their hunger and the hopelessness of their position, there was no collapse, as long as they believed Manstein was on his way. Even when that hope withered, the Army faded away rather than cracked. During December about 80,000 men, one

The beginning of the end

142

143

quarter of the encircled force, were lost from wounds, hunger and sickness, but the remainder continued to fight, and the Soviet Don Front commander, General Rokossovsky, decided that a set-piece operation would be needed to reduce them.

The main attack would be delivered from the west by Batov's 65th and Chistyakov's 21st Armies, who would aim to split the encircled force. The 66th (Zhadov) and 24th (Galanin) Armies would attack simultaneously from the north while 57th (Tolbukhin) and 64th (Shumilov) came in from the south. The 62nd Army was assigned the task of keeping the Germans busy enough so that they could not withdraw forces to cope with the other Armies' attacks, and of stopping any attempt by them to retreat across the frozen Volga. The date of the attack was set for January 10th, 1943.

However the Stavka Representative, Colonel-General of Artillery Voronov, and Rokossovsky decided first to try the effect of an offer of honourable capitulation, so on January 8th they sent representatives to the German lines under a flag of truce. The offer, typed on Stavka notepaper, was an interesting blend of 20th Century psychological warfare and 18th-Century military punctilio. It read:

'TO THE COMMANDER OF VI GERMAN ARMY SURROUNDED AT STALINGRAD, COLONEL-GENERAL PAULUS, OR HIS REPRESENTATIVE.

'The VI German Army, formations of IV Panzer Army, and attached reinforcement units have been completely encircled since 23rd November, 1942. Units of the Red Army had surrounded this group of German forces with a solid ring. All hopes of rescue of your forces by an attack by German troops from the South and South-West have proved unjustified. The German forces which hastened to your aid have been smashed by the Red Army, and remnants of those forces are retreating towards Rostov. The German transport air force, which is bringing you starvation rations of food, ammunition, and fuel has been compelled to change its airfields frequently because of the successful swift advance of the Red Army and to fly to the positions of the encircled

Left above: Only a fortunate few were to escape. *Left below:* Bad weather grounded the majority of the Luftwaffe. *Above:* No escape

troops from a long distance. In addition to this the German transport air force is suffering immense losses in aircraft and crews from the Russian Air Force. Its assistance to the encircled troops is becoming fictitious.

'The situation of the encircled troops is serious. They are suffering hunger, sickness, and cold. The severe Russian winter is only beginning; hard frosts, cold winds and blizzards are still to come, and your soldiers have not been provided with winter uniforms and find themselves in severe, unhealthy conditions.

'You as the Commander, and all officers of the encircled forces understand very well that you have no real possibilities of breaking the ring of encirclement. Your situation is hopeless and further resistance is completely pointless.

'In view of your hopeless position, and to avoid senseless bloodshed, we propose that you accept the following terms of capitulation;

'1. All the encircled German forces headed by you and your staff to cease resistance.

'2. You to hand over to us all personnel, armaments, all military equipment and military property in working order.

'We guarantee to all officers, NCOs, and men who cease resistance their lives and safety, and after the end of

145

the war return to Germany or to any country to which the prisoners express a desire to go.

'All personnel of forces which surrender may retain their military uniform, badges of rank and medals, personal effects, valuables, and in the case of senior officers, their swords.

'Normal rations will be instituted immediately for all officers, NCOs and men who surrender. Medical aid will be given to all wounded, sick, and frost-bitten.

'Your reply is expected at 1500 hours Moscow time on January 9th, 1943 in written form by a representative personally appointed by you, who must drive in a light vehicle with a white flag along the road from Konny siding to Kotluban station.

'Your representative will be met by authorised Russian officers in area 'B' 0.5 km South-East of siding 564 at 1500 hours on January 9th, 1943.

'In the event our proposal for capitulation is refused by you, we warn you that forces of the Red Army and Red Air Fleet will be compelled to take the matter to annihilation of the encircled German forces, and for their destruction you will bear the responsibility.'

The ultimatum was signed by Voronov on behalf of Stvka and by Rokossovsky as C-in-C Don Front, and was one of considerable psychological persuasiveness, with its references to the horrors of winter still to come, its cold but accurate description (verifiable as such by Paulus) of the failure of the relief expedition, the promise of food and medical treatment and the old-fashioned touch, echoing Grant's surrender terms to Lee at Appomattox in 1865, and appealing to the traditional sense of military courtesy 'senior officers may keep their swords'. To redouble its effect on morale, copies of it were dropped to Paulus' troops.

But however persuasive the terms, Paulus was not yet disposed to give up, or perhaps was not sufficiently strong-willed to overrule the determined Schmidt, so the terms were rejected, and Voronov set about fulfilling the threat in the last paragraph of the ultimatum. He wanted a quick end to

the business, for the seven armies tied up at Stalingrad could be better used elsewhere in developing the offensive into a total shattering of the German front in the south. Operation 'Ring', the dissection and annihilation of VI Army and its attached units, was to go forward.

It was a carefully planned operation, for The Red Army's senior commanders had a healthy respect for the German soldier which imposed on their planning a cautious concern for the practicable, which Hitler's generals frequently found it necessary or expedient to ignore. The Fuhrer constantly demanded miracles from his troops, and frequently got them, but Stavka, as befitted the instruments of an avowedly atheistic régime, tended to eschew the supernatural.

For Operation 'Ring' they had seven armies, whereas Paulus had the equivalent of two (VI, most of IV

Far left: Supplies down to the occasional parachute drop. *Centre:* Food or ammunition? *Below:* Wire for the last defence!

Panzer, numerous individual units, two Rumanian infantry divisions, and a battalion of Croat separatists). But a Soviet army was about equivalent in size to a German corps, and two of the armies (62nd and 64th) were much below strength. The Germans actually had slightly more men and tanks in the pocket than did the force encircling it, though the Red Army had a superiority in artillery of three to two, and in aircraft of three to one.

But there was a world of difference between the well-clad, properly fed troops of Don Front, with the scent of victory in their nostrils, and the cold, hungry and ill-clad soldiers of VI Army, just as the T-34s of Rokossovsky's mobile forces, properly supplied with fuel and ammunition, could not be compared with the German Mk III and IV tanks, almost immobile and almost impotent for lack of both. Nevertheless, Voronov took no risks, and the operation was conducted as carefully as if the Germans were fresh and unweakened.

He opened the proceedings at 0805 hours on the morning of January 10th, with a fifty-five minute bombardment by thousands of guns and mortars and hundreds of aircraft; then, at 0900 hours precisely, the storming of Stalingrad began with an attack across the city from Vertyachi towards the 'Red October' factory aimed at splitting Paulus' force in two. At the same time secondary attacks were put in from Tsybenko to Basargino station and from Yerzovka towards Gorodishche.

Once more the tortured soil of Stalingrad heaved under the explosion of bomb and shell, and the familiar names of months back – the Rossoshka river, Pitomnik, the Tsaritsa – crept back into the communiques. But this time the sequence was like a speeded-up film, for where in the autumn Paulus was using divisions, and fighting against well-fed troops, Voronov was using armies and fighting a starving, freezing and demoralised enemy, without food, ammunition, or hope. In the circumstances it was a tribute to the German soldier that he would still fight at all, but fight he did, though he knew his cause was lost.

Even so, it was not to be expected

147

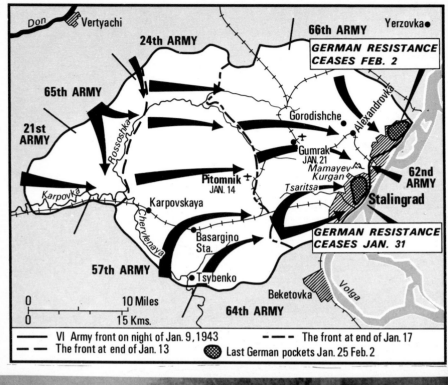

Don Vertyachi

24th ARMY

66th ARMY Yerzovka

GERMAN RESISTANCE CEASES FEB. 2

65th ARMY

21st ARMY

Rossoshka

Gorodishche

Alexandrovka

Gumrak
JAN. 21

Mamayev Kurgan

62nd ARMY

Karpovka

Pitomnik
JAN. 14

Tsaritsa

Stalingrad

Karpovskaya

Chervlenaya

Basargino Sta.

GERMAN RESISTANCE CEASES JAN. 31

57th ARMY

Tsybenko

Beketovka

Volga

0 — 10 Miles
0 — 15 Kms.

64th ARMY

—— VI Army front on night of Jan. 9, 1943 — ▪ — The front at end of Jan. 17
— — — The front at end of Jan. 13   ▨ Last German pockets Jan. 25 Feb. 2

Storming through the ruins

that he could repel the Soviet onslaught. What had taken Paulus weeks to capture, Voronov and Rokossovsky regained in days. The main force (the whole of 65th Army plus the striking forces of 21st and 24th) reached the west bank of the Rossoshka on the 13th, the Germans were pushed back from the Chervlenaya river, and on the 14th lost their main supply airfield at Pitomnik. By evening of the 16th the German-held perimeter had been reduced from about five hundred and fifty square miles to less than two hundred and fifty. For supply there remained only the subsidiary airfield at Gumrak; and if the Luftwaffe had been unable to meet even the starvation minimum of three hundred tons a day (there had never been any chance that they could supply the six hundred tons necessary for proper sustenance of the besieged garrison, and their best performance was the delivery of two hundred and eighty nine tons in one day) with two airfields, there was not a hope that VI Army could be kept going with only Gumrak available.

Plan of attack

The scenes at the airfields beggared description in those January days. An aircraft would land, bumping its way over the snow-covered runway, and unloading would go on at high speed, because the Soviet artillery frequently bombarded the area, Soviet fighters swooped overhead ready to pick off the unwieldy German transports as they came and went, and roving groups of T-34s periodically shot up the airfield. Then the loading would begin, while harassed Movement Control officers and *Feldgendarmerie*, frequently with drawn pistols, attempted to sort out the genuinely entitled from the deserters – the bandaged officer who turned out to have no wound underneath the dressing on his arm, the Colonel who had written his own documents ordering himself to fly out to Army Group Don 'for special duties', or the sergeant with the self-inflicted wound.

Meanwhile, the stretcher-borne wounded waited helplessly to be loaded, wondering, if still capable of thought, whether they would get aboard at all, and whether, if they did, they would survive the packs of Soviet fighters and the hundreds of heavy anti-aircraft guns which the Red Army had installed on the steppe along their route. Then all would be ready; the aircraft would jolt its way to the end of the runway, gather speed and lumber into the air, in at least two instances with a panic-stricken wretch still hanging to the tailplane until within minutes his frozen hands relaxed their grip and he fell to his death.

That was the reality behind the bombastic utterances of the Nazi radio, and the military communiques with their references to 'stubborn resistance against overwhelmingly superior forces'. In the front line, the infantry fought stolidly on, but behind them the organism was rotting. They were the shell on the egg, concealing the fact that the inside has gone bad; and like the eggshell, they were about to be cracked. Voronov and Rokossovky were already planning how to crack them, by putting into effect the second and final phase of Operation Ring.

By the evening of the 17th the Germans were back on the inner defensive perimeter of the city itself, and an uneasy lull began while Don Front regrouped for the last push. Gumrak airfield fell into Soviet hands on the 21st, and the final stage of Operation Ring began on the following day. The main parts were played by the infantry and massed artillery, particularly the latter – on the front occupied by 21st, 57th, and 64th Armies there was a gun or mortar every six yards for fourteen miles – four thousand one hundred of them.

No army could stand up for long to this weight of attack, and by the 25th Don Front had reached the centre of Stalingrad. At the 'Red October' housing estate and on the Mamayev Kurgan Chistyakov's tanks of 21st Army suddenly found not Germans but

The airfield recaptured **with Luftwaffe planes grounded**

Soviet troops ahead of them. The 62nd Army's main force was no longer isolated from Don Front.

Now Paulus occupied an area of only thirtysix square miles, and his force was split into two as Chuykov's had been for so many weeks. Its destruction was a matter of days.

Both German and Soviet generals and military theorists agree that up

to about January 24th, VI Army was performing a useful service to Germany by tying down the Soviet armies there – in particular Yeremenko's offensive towards Rostov was starved of troops because of the continued resistance of VI Army, and he failed to achieve his objective of cutting off Army Group A's retreat from the Caucasus. But by the 24th it was clear that Army Group A was going to make its escape through Rostov, and that VI Army, whose last airfield, Gumrak, had fallen three days previously, was in any case no longer capable of tying down Soviet forces of any size.

Some commanding officers had begun to negotiate the individual surrenders of their units with the opposing forces, despite orders to the contrary, and there was no point in further resistance. At 1645 hours on the 24th Manstein received a signal from VI Army which reported, among other things '. . . Frightful conditions in the city area proper, where about twenty thousand unattended wounded are seeking shelter in the ruins. With them are about the same number of starved and frost-bitten men, and stragglers, mostly without weapons . . . Last resistance on city outskirts in southern part of Stalingrad will be offered on January 25th . . . Tractor Factory may perhaps hold out a little longer . . .'

Manstein made a last attempt by telephone to persuade Hitler to allow a surrender, but in vain. Major Zitzewitz, the OKH liaison officer in Stalingrad had been flown out in one of the last aircraft to leave Gumrak on the 20th, and on the 23rd had made a similar attempt in a personal interview with the Führer. But Hitler was by now completely out of touch with reality, and was talking of sending a single battalion of the new (and untried) Panther medium tanks through the hundred miles and more of Soviet-controlled territory between Army Group Don and Stalingrad to open a corridor. Zitzewitz was flabbergasted, but he did his best to bring Hitler back to earth. He spoke of hunger, frostbite, lack of supplies, the untended wounded, and ended with the blunt statement 'the troops at Stalingrad can no longer be ordered to fight to the last round because they are no longer physically able to fight and no longer have a last round'.

Hitler looked through him. 'Man recovers very quickly' he said, and sent a radio message to Paulus. 'Surrender is forbidden. VI Army will hold its positions to the last man and the last round, and by their heroic endurance will make an unforgettable contribution to the establishment of a defensive front and the salvation of the western world.'

So VI Army was sent to its doom with a sordid lie. It was no longer making any contribution, unforgettable or otherwise, to the establishment of a defensive front. Nor, come to that, could the people of occupied Western Europe be readily expected to view the regime which had destroyed their freedom and independence in 1939 and 1940 as contributing to the 'salvation of the western world.'

Paulus had had to move his headquarters from Gumrak when the Soviets overran it, and had installed himself and his staff in the basement of a large department store, the 'Univermag', on the western outskirts of the city. On January 30th this fact became known to General Shumilov of 64th Army, in whose sector it was, and he at once organised a mobile detachment of tanks and motorised infantry from 38th Motorised Brigade, adding an engineer battalion whose job was to clear the mines around the store. With the detachment was the Intelligence Officer of the Brigade, Senior Lieutenant Ilchenko. By 0600 hours on the 31st they had surrounded the store and began shelling it.

After a few minutes a German Officer came out of the side door and motioned for an officer to come over. Ilchenko crossed the street, and the officer said 'Our boss wants to talk to your boss'.

'Our boss is busy. You'll have to deal with me' said Ilchenko, and with two of his soldiers was taken down to the basement, where they met Schmidt and Major-General Rosske of Paulus' staff. Rosske said that the surrender would be negotiated only with representatives of the Front or Army command. Ilchenko reported this by radio to Shumilov, who at once sent his Chiefs of Operations and Intelli-

gence, Colonels Lukin and Ryzhov. On arrival they negotiated first with Rosske then with Schmidt, who said 'Paulus has not been answerable for anything since yesterday', though from time to time they disappeared into the room where he lay chain smoking and twitching nervously, on his bed. Paulus' staff refused to negotiate the surrender of the northern group, which was now under the command of General Strecker, and as for the southern group they agreed to its capitulation but pointed out that they had no means of delivering the order to their troops.

It was finally agreed that the order would be delivered by officers from each army, and Colonels Ryzhov and Mutovin of 64th Army staff were designated to accompany the German staff officers on this task. Only after they had left was Colonel Lukin taken to see Paulus. The VI Army HQ was given one hour to pack up, and while they were doing so Shumilov's Chief-of-Staff, Major-General Laskin, arrived to conduct Paulus and Schmidt to Shumilov's headquarters at Beketovka.

Shumilov awaited their arrival with impatience and curiosity. At last the door opened and a tall, grey-haired man in the uniform of a Colonel-General entered the room. He raised his arm from, force of habit, in the Nazi salute, then sheepishly lowered it and said 'Good day' instead of Heil Hitler.

Austerely Shumilov asked for his identity documents. Paulus felt in his pockets and produced his service book. Shumilov, determined to take no chances examined it and then asked for documents certifying that Paulus was the C-in-C of VI Army. Fortunately Paulus had that, too (Shumilov does not say what he would have done if Paulus hadn't), and finally the punctilious commander of 64th Army asked whether the reports that he had been promoted to Field-Marshal were true. (They were; Hitler had promoted him in the hope that this would encourage him to die fighting.)

Schmidt had been listening with growing impatience to the conversation, and could no longer bear to be excluded from it. With a pride not perhaps entirely appropriate to the

**The surrender of Field-Marshal Paulus
.. and his army**

circumstances he announced in a ceremonious tone, 'Yesterday, by order of the Fuhrer, the rank of General Field-Marshal, the highest in the Reich, was conferred upon Colonel General von Paulus'.

Shumilov believed a Chief-of-Staff should speak when spoken to, and turned back to Paulus. 'Then I may report to Stavka', he said 'that *Field-Marshal* Paulus has been taken prisoner by troops of my Army?'

'*Jawohl*', came the answer.

During the official interrogation which followed, Paulus' spirits began to pick up, when he realised that he could expect civilised treatment from his captors, and by the time lunch was served he was happier than he had been for weeks. He called for vodka, poured a glass for each of his staff officers, and proposed a toast. 'To those who defeated us, the Russian Army and its leaders'. All rose and drank.

General Strecker's northern group lasted only a little while longer, and under pressure from 62nd, 65th, and 66th Armies it too capitulated, on February 2nd 1943. There were three days of national mourning in Germany and for some weeks even Hitler appeared to have lost faith in his military genius, so that Manstein enjoyed for a brief period a freedom of action which few German generals had had that year. He made good use of it, inflicting a serious reverse on the over-extended armies of Golikov and Vatutin, and recovering much of the lost ground north of the Don. But the Stalingrad campaign really ended on February 2nd, 1943, since no subsequent tactical victory could erase what had happened on the bank of the Volga.

The military importance of the victory can be expressed partly in figures. Almost the whole of five Axis armies had been wiped out by the time the thaw came – all of VI Army, most of IV Panzer Army, five out of seven divisions of III Rumanian, almost all of IV Rumanian and of VIII Italian Armies. Some thirty-two divisions and three brigades were completely shattered, and a further sixteen

153

divisions lost more than half their personnel, while many more had to abandon much of their heavy equipment to get away. Total Axis casualties in killed, wounded, missing, or captured will never be known with absolute certainty, but they were in the neighbourhood of one million five hundred thousand between August 1942 and February 1943, while about three thousand five hundred tanks and assault guns (about seven months production) were lost, with over half a year's output of guns and mortars (about twelve thousand), and three thousand aircraft (at least four months' production). Altogether the equipment lost between August and February would suffice to equip approximately seventy-five divisions.

Yet the figures tell only part of the story. German generals could rationalise the defeat, as they had the one at Moscow, by pointing to various errors made by Hitler, and after the war many of them were to fight the battle over again in their memoirs, this time winning it. If Halder's original plan had been followed; if Kleist and Ruoff had been set in motion later, so that they and Hoth could have got round South Front instead of simply herding it away to the Caucasus; if Hoth had not been sent south to help Kleist, who needed no help; if Hitler had not diverted divisions back to the West; if all these things, and others had been done differently, then the outcome would have been different.

But there is one fatal flaw in this type of reasoning; when examined closely the enemy is always assumed to be doing what he actually did, whereas in real life, each side's actions are to some extent determined by those of its adversary. If the Germans had behaved differently, the Stavka reactions would also have been different; and Stavka made its mistakes too, the most obvious one being the mounting of the Kharkov offensive in May, The historian, writing after the event, has information which the general conducting the battle did not have at the time, and any battle, but particularly one of the scale and complexity of Stalingrad, is a dynamic event, in which decisions have to be taken frequently, quickly, and on incomplete information. In the nature of things, a proportion of them will inevitably be wrong, some of them disastrously so. And all that can be said is that the decisions taken by the Soviet generals were more often right than those of the Germans, and fewer of the wrong ones were disastrouly wrong.

Taking the general picture, therefore, the flexibility and imaginativeness of the Soviet defence, and the boldness of the counteroffensive plan conceived and executed primarily by Zhukov and Vasilevsky, was a product of high military skill, when compared with the dull mincing-machine approach adopted by the commanders of Army Group B and VI Army, and it was superior generalship, not superiority in numbers which decided the issue. Insofar as the Stavka gambled, it gambled successfully, first on its ability to maintain 62nd Army in its isolated position, and secondly on being able to assemble the large strike forces for the counteroffensive without attracting the attention of the Germans. The German leaders, on the other hand, gambled on their ability to remove a nation with twice Germany's manpower potential from the list of combatants in a matter of months, and that they came so near to success is a tribute to their skill in excution rather than a commendation of their judgement in selecting such an objective in the first place.

The Soviet side, too, has its disputes, but on a more personal level, as to whether the 'Southern generals' or the 'Muscovites' were the more responsible for the victory. In Stalin's time, this kind of argument could not arise, since all success flowed from his genius. But once he had left the scene the arguments broke out with all the more fury for having been pent up for ten years. Khrushchev had been in the south ever since the beginning of the war, and felt the odium attached to the 'Southern generals' reflected upon himself.

It is a fact that of the generals posted to the Stalingrad area to restore the situation were a number who had held high posts in the battle of Moscow – Zhukov, Vasilevsky, Yeremenko, Golikov, Vatutin, Rokossovsky, G F Zakharov (Yeremenko's Chief of Staff), Batov (65th Army), Zhadov (66th Army), and that these men took leading roles; Zhukov, the supreme director, and all the Front commanders having actually held field command in the Moscow battle. During the ascendancy of Khrushchev, the role of these men was played down, and the importance of the 'locals', especially Khrushchev, being exaggerated.

One name which has not so far been mentioned at all so far is that of Georgy Malenkov who, as a member of Stalin's secretariat, spent much time on the spot, and probably played a more important part than Khrushchev in keeping Stalin informed and ensuring that the Party machinery was mobilised behind the Stalingrad operation. Yet little or nothing is known about his time there, because his fall from power in 1955 has made him a non-person whose name is almost never mentioned, and whose presence at Stalingrad is ignored.

However, it is clear that the leading role in preparing the 'trap' and then springing it was Zhukov's. As Deputy Supreme Commander he was the senior soldier concerned with the operation, and he was certainly no figurehead in this or any of his other battles before or after. The 62nd Army was the cheese in the trap, and Chuykov's handling of it, particularly in the development of small-formation tactics to suit the unique conditions (there had never been a siege *inside* a city of comparable scale and duration) made it possible for 62nd Army to retain its foothold and therefore to hold the large German force in its vulnerable forward position long enough for the counteroffensive force to be assembled. Equally, without Yeremenko's frantic but inspired improvisations on August 23rd, it is doubtful whether 62nd Army would have had time to develop the tactics which it so successfully employed against German forces with. local superiority, especially in the air.

Soviet sources publish only very scanty data about the Red Army's own losses, but it is clear that they were considerably less than those of the Germans, as German figures show no big 'round-up' of Soviet troops at any time 1942 after May, few of the Soviet wounded fell into German hands, casualties from cold or hunger were negligible by comparison with those of the Germans, and the only major attrition was among the divisions sent into Stalingrad. Losses among these were at times very heavy, but most of the wounded were evacuated across the Volga where presumably most of them stood a good chance of recovery. As to the killed, the removal for reburial of corpses buried in the city produced one hundred and forty seven thousand two hundred German and forty six thousand seven hundred Soviet dead.

Of the three hundred and thirty thousand surrounded within the original perimeter (of which the city area formed only a small part), only ninety one thousand marched out after the capitulation. These men were already in a very weak state from cold and lack of food. and tyhpus had already made its appearance shortly before the surrender. After the men had been moved to temporary prisoner of war camps in the Beketovka-Krasnoarmeysk area, a typhus epidemic broke out, killing about fifty thousand of the enfeebled survivors, and of the remainder many thousands died while being marched to camps in the hinterland, mostly in Central Asia. The German prisoners were put to forced labour, and the last of them returned only in 1955. Altogether only five thousand of the original ninety one thousand prisoners ever saw Germany again.

And what did Hitler think of it all? He was dumbfounded at the surrender, and prophesied that the Generals would be tortured and made to give anti-Nazi broadcasts over Moscow Radio. They made the broadcasts all right, though it does not appear that they were in fact tortured – at least none of those who returned after the war made any allegation of serious ill-treatment. Some twenty four Generals went into captivity, and unlike their men, most of them survived the war. Paulus was an active member of the anti-Nazi 'Free Officers' Committee', though he had so much of the courtier in his make-up that it is impossible to tell whether he had 'seen the light' or adapted himself to serve a new master – perhaps the latter, as after the war he elected to live in the Soviet Zone of Germany.

Apart from the military consequences of the defeat – the most striking of which was the permanent change in the manpower balance, which developed so that whereas in November 1942 the Red Army began its counteroffensive on a basis of roughly parity, seven and a half months later, when it began the battle of Kursk, it had a superiority in manpower of over two to one – there were important political effects too. In Munich, the birthplace of the Nazi movement, rioting broke out among the students, and, though it was brutally suppressed, it showed that some cracks had begun to appear in the fasade of German unity behind Hitler.

Henceforward, a German soldier sent to the Eastern Front was both a hero and martyr. In the Asia Minor Middle East area, any German hope of inveigling Turkey into the war on the side of the Axis faded away in the strong light of reality, as did the heady dreams of taking the British in the rear, cutting off the Allied Middle East oil supplies at source, or stopping

the flow of supplies to Russia through Iran.

But the supreme irony was that Germany was able to go on fighting for another two years and three months after that fatal February day in Stalingrad. Though she never succeeded in laying her hands on the oil of the Caucasus, the success of her industrial chemists in manufacturing petrol from coal enabled her to keep her armies and her economy going, though admittedly not without crippling shortages, caused more by Allied bombing of the refineries than by lack of raw materials or refining capacity. Hitler's apprehensions about his own oil supply, which had led him to urge his armies on beyond the relatively simpler task of disrupting *Soviet* oil supply, and to a fatal division of force which gained them neither the Caucasus nor the Volga, had been exaggerated.

So, in the end, it had all been unnecessary . . .

Bibliography

The Year of Stalingrad Alexander Werth (Hamish Hamilton, London. Knopf, New York)
Russia At War 1941-1945 Alexander Werth (Barrie and Rockliffe, London. Dutton, New York)
Juggernaut Malcolm Mackintosh (Secker & Warburg, London. The Macmillan Co, New York)
Hitler's War on Russia (US: *Hitler Moves East* 1941-1943) Paul Carell (Little, Brown. Boston. Harrap, London)
Stalingrad Yeremenko (Moscow)
Barbarossa Alan Clark (Hutchinson, London. Morrow, New York)
The Beginning of The Road (US: *The Battle for Stalingrad*) Vasili Chiukov (Holt, London. Rinehart & Winston, New York)
A History of Russia Nicholas V Riasonovsky (Oxford University Press, Oxford & New York)
The Soviet Army ed B H Liddell Hart (Weidenfeld & Nicholson, London)
A History of the Soviet Army Michel Garder (Pall Mall Press, London)
Halder's Diaries (English Translation in manuscript at Office of Chief of Military History, Department of the Army, Washington)
Inside Hitler's Headquarters, 1939-45 General Walter Warlimont (Weidenfeld & Nicholson, London)